It Happened In New York City

D0878268

It Happened In Series

It Happened In New York City

Remarkable Events That Shaped History

Fran Capo and
Art & Susan Zuckerman

gpp

Guilford, Connecticut

To buy books in quantity for corporate use
or incentives, call **(800) 962-0973**
or e-mail **premiums@GlobePequot.com.**

Copyright © 2010 by Morris Book Publishing, LLC

ALL RIGHTS RESERVED. No part of this book may be reproduced or transmitted in any form by any means, electronic or mechanical, including photocopying and recording, or by any information storage and retrieval system, except as may be expressly permitted in writing from the publisher. Requests for permission should be addressed to Globe Pequot Press, Attn: Rights and Permissions Department, P.O. Box 480, Guilford, CT 06437.

Project editor: David Legere
Map: Daniel Lloyd © Morris Book Publishing, LLC

Library of Congress Cataloging-in-Publication Data
Capo, Fran, 1959-
  It happened in New York City : remarkable events that shaped history / Fran Capo and Art and Susan Zuckerman.
      p. cm.
  Includes bibliographical references and index.
  ISBN 978-0-7627-5421-2
  1. New York (N.Y.)—History—Anecdotes. 2. New York (N.Y.)—Biography—Anecdotes. 3. New York (N.Y.)—Social life and customs—Anecdotes. I. Zuckerman, Art. II. Zuckerman, Susan. III. Title.
  F128.36.C37 2010
  974.7'1—dc22
                                    2009038605

Printed in the United States of America

10 9 8 7 6 5 4 3 2 1

Fran: In memory of my mom, Rose Capo, a true New Yorker,
who taught me that nothing is impossible.

Art and Sue: To our sons, Mark and Scott, for their understanding, to
all our friends who we dragged with us in the beginning, and to the
teachers and our tour guests who forced us to never stop learning.

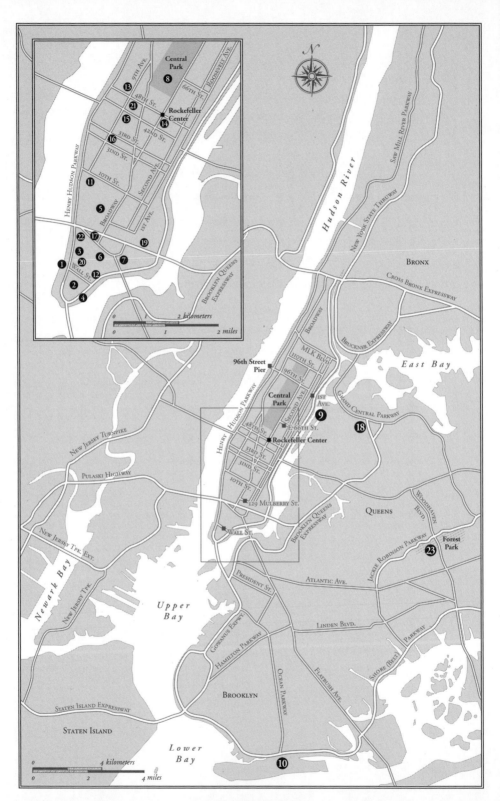

NEW YORK CITY

LEGEND

Note to Reader:

Although most New Yorkers refer to Manhattan as New York City, or the "City," New York City is actually composed of five boroughs: Manhattan, Queens, Brooklyn, The Bronx, and Staten Island. This book covers bits of history for all of New York City.

CONTENTS

CONTENTS

FRAN'S ACKNOWLEDGMENTS

This is my fourth book in the *It Happened in* series and I'm glad once again to have uncovered some pretty cool, little-known stories about New York City. I could have taken the easy route and retold some of the stories from *It Happened in New York,* but I wanted to bring you new things to talk about with your friends at the next family barbecue. Things that would make you want to explore New York City a little closer. Things that would make you win a trivia game, things that make your friends say, "Wow, how do you know so much?"

On this book writing journey, I was happy that I was able to invite two talented friends along as coauthors, Art and Susan Zuckerman. Since there were three of us, we each wrote several chapters . . . seemed the fair thing to do. We decided collectively as a team what to write, and then picked our favorites. They are a wealth of knowledge on New York City, and I have done "celebrity fast talking" tours with them about New York City with their tour company, Z Travel and Leisure. So I thought who better to write this book with. Thanks, Art and Susan, for sharing the coauthorship of this book with me, made it a whole lot easier.

Or course I had help as any good author does along the way, so I'd like to thank Matt Henry for supplying the raging bull flyer and www.StatenIslandChat.com and its editor for being of such help. My friends once again at the Queens Borough Library for always helping me find the right sources. Globe Pequot, for once again asking me to write another book for them, and my editors, Erin Turner and Meredith Davis, who let me run wild when it comes to publicity.

And of course to the people in my life who put up with my long hours of writing (and wild adventures). My incredible fiancé, Steve (who calls me relentlessly relentless in all I do and who always buys the first copy of my books . . . all I can say is now there's a guy who deserves . . . a lot!), my fantastic son, Spencer (who always tells me I'm doing a great job), my adorable niece, Athena (who now at the age of nine wants to become a writer and brings all my books to her school); my nutty but lovable sister, Shahira, and Donna Drake, my wonderful friend and co-host of our new television show, *Live it Up! With Donna Drake and Fran Capo,* who worked around my writing schedule for our television taping and is launching us to new success. Also want to thank my best friend, Janette Barber, for always being a funny and honest listening ear and for putting our "Just Talkin' with Fran and Janette" project on hold until I got everything done. Also my friends, Viv Maltese (who I did my first adventures with), Jeanie and Joe Otero (who always come to my book signings and give them as gifts to friends), Nik Halik (who gave me a break from writing by sending me to Antarctica to get chased by a leopard seal and then asking me to do my "Dare to Do It" talks and then wrote about it in his book, *Thrillionaire*), Lisa Wernick (who hired me for my first voiceover and is part of my sister club), Pat Riches, John Basedow (who I do a series of talks with called "Success Made Simple" and for always being enthusiastic with everything I do), Steve Maraboli (who is introducing me to his listening audience and publishing my book, *Hopeville: The City of Light*), and Saranne Rothberg of *Comedy Cures Laugh Talk Radio,* whom I co-host a national radio show with, for being excited about my TV show, this new book, and for promoting it on the radio and giving me time off to write and do what I needed to do.

Lastly, my friends Dale Kilian (who watches out for my niece Athena while I'm working), Alli Berman (for always being ready to relax me with her paintings), Natalie Weinstein (who put all my nice stuff into Steve's house, so that I would move in and have a nicer place to write), Beth Bogush (for working on my Capo cartoon with me that will show some of these New York places), Ellen Easton (who always promotes my books), Rick Morgan (who always brags about my books on stage), Dawn Vaccaro (who lets me know my mom is watching and knows I've done another book), Mark Shepard, for helping me break a fifth world record for our song, "Adventure Girl" in the midst of me writing this book, Lynn Prowse for letting me do a teleseminar on the book, Kim Orlando of http://travelingmom.com, Wanda Mauro and family—Vanessa, William, and Isabel (who always feed my son and cats when I'm gone), Catherine Wright, Charles and Luis, Arron, Rachel, Camille, and Jude (for always offering to lighten the workload), Margaret for watching things while I'm gone, Jamie, Lisa Davis, Jeff Unger, Gracie, Chelsea, Joe and Shereen Randazza (for lending me an emergency locator beacon while in Antarctica so I could come home safe and write the rest of my book).

Carson Tang, Jan Turner, Nancy Lombardo, Jeff at Nighsky-murals, Bea Davis, Manny Yarbrough, Gemini, Barry Brown, Marvin Soskil, Heidi Adams, Laurie Caso, Denise DiStephan, and to Throwdini, Dean Gould, Ashrita, and all my world-record friends who said they will Tweet this book when it's done. I have to say I am truly lucky to have a trillion dollars worth of friends. Hey, if the national budget can be that high, I can have that vested in my wonderful friends. I am truly blessed. Thanks, guys. Spread the word about the book!

Finally thanks to Mother Mary for always answering my prayers. And now without hogging up the whole intro . . . Art and Susan have something to say (they really are two people). Hit it, guys.

ART AND SUE'S ACKNOWLEDGMENTS

Hi! Art and Susan here. (Fran, could you have talked faster above?) Anyway, we would like to thank Fran Capo, who has helped us to create a seven-hour tour in fifteen minutes and is the hardest working person we have ever met and for bringing us on as co-authors in this book.

On our quest for knowledge we would like to say that Alfred Pommer has been our walking encyclopedia, and Stephen Duer has helped guide us through the five boroughs and showed us things in a different light.

Bladavesta Magegevski's help on the *Panorama* was immeasurable.

Josephine LaFauci has inspired us with her motivation and her enthusiasm.

We would also like to acknowledge Teddy and Misty, our two golden retrievers, who always patiently wait for us to come home and have spent many a late night as companions when we were up writing.

And finally, we would like to acknowledge all the teachers whom we have met over the past several years who have inspired us to keep on learning new things about New York City. We appreciate their thirst for knowledge and the challenges that they present us to always learn more.

And finally, finally . . . from all of us . . . if you like this book . . . spread the word; we are nowhere without the help of our readers!

PIRATES, HIJACKED JEWS, AND THE WALL

1654

A small wooden ship carefully glided along the wharf of the little hamlet of New Amsterdam. Its sails were lowered to prevent it from being swept on the rocks by the water's treacherous current. On the front of the ship stood a tanned man with a full head of prematurely gray hair and beard to match. He looked haggard. Yet his eyes seemed to sparkle. He lifted his arms to the heavens and seemed to be murmuring to himself as the ship made its way into the dock. The man was Asser Levy and the year was 1654. Levy and his twenty-two Jewish companions had just completed a harrowing journey from Recife in Brazil to the Dutch colony that was the anchor of the great Dutch West India Company's empire in North America. New Amsterdam was not their intended destination, but fate had intervened and brought them here.

When Asser Levy and the other Jews landed in New Amsterdam in 1654, they did not know what to expect. Would they be allowed to live in peace in this isolated colony, or would they be persecuted just as they, and generations of Jews before them, had suffered? Little did they know what was to follow! As Asser looked out over his new "home," he could not help but think back to how he and his little band had arrived at this place.

It had all begun for his people in the 1400s during the notorious Inquisition in Spain. During this period, Torquemada, the Grand High Inquisitor under the rule of King Ferdinand and Queen Isabella, tortured, killed, and exiled thousands of Jews who were unwilling to renounce their faith. Spanish rulers invoked religious laws based on "purity of blood." Jews who had professed to renounce their religion and converted to Catholicism became known as "Marranos" (Spanish for pigs) because of their refusal to eat pork.

Many Jews fled to various safe havens. Luckily for them, their neighbor Portugal in the 1490s was very tolerant to the Jews who lived within their boundaries. Unfortunately, this all changed when the daughter of King Ferdinand and Queen Isabella of Spain became engaged to Manuel, the son of Portugal's King John. The Spanish princess refused to marry the Portuguese prince unless the "infidel" Jews were exiled from Portugal. Wanting the princess as his wife, the prince began a new, and even more horrible, Inquisition, and the Jews were once again forced to flee.

This time many of them fled to Brazil, which was under the control of the Dutch at that time. Here the Jews coexisted peacefully for one hundred sixty years. Then in 1653, after a long and bloody battle, parts of Dutch Brazil, especially Recife, were seized by the Portuguese and the persecution began all over again. After the take-over, the Jews were ordered out of Brazil. Fortunately, the leader of the Portuguese, General Francisco Barreto, gave the Jewish colony three months to get their affairs in order and leave. He also sent a message to his soldiers not to persecute the "children of Israel" or else they would be punished severely.

Asser Levy and his family gathered their belongings and set their affairs in order. Then Levy, who was a born leader and organizer, contracted a ship to take his family and three other families to Amsterdam, which was one of the few cities in the world where Jews were accepted as equal citizens. In the early spring of 1654, sixteen ships full of expelled Jews left the Brazilian colony of Recife. Fifteen of them sailed on to safe ports, mostly in the Netherlands and the Caribbean, but the sixteenth ship, the one carrying Asser and his family, suffered a different fate. Blown off course and separated from their countrymen, their ship was captured by Spanish pirates. Asser Levy stood helplessly by as he and the other passengers and crew were taken prisoner. He watched as their ship was set afire and sunk. The pirates confiscated the personal belongings of the twenty-three Sephardic Jews (four men, six women, and thirteen children), which they hoped would bring a good price. But Asser knew that a worse fate than losing their possessions lay ahead. They were to be dropped off at the nearest Caribbean port and sold as slaves.

For weeks Levy and the other Jewish prisoners were at the mercy of the pirates. Then, one fateful day, Asser and his companions, confined to the hold of the ship, heard a terrible commotion coming from the deck. The pirate ship was being attacked by a French warship under the command of Jacques de la Motthe. To the relief of the Jews, they were rescued by the French. They were taken onboard the vessel *The St. Catherine,* along with their possessions. Asser and the others were grateful to their rescuers. However, Asser sensed that Captain de la Motthe was not thrilled with the unwelcomed "guests" on his ship. He was not caring for them out of the goodness of his heart. He just wanted money from the "well-off Jews" for their passage, and he and his crew would be on their way. The French captain's plan was to drop them off at a hamlet described as "the end of the inhabited earth," otherwise known as New Amsterdam.

When the ship docked in late August on the New Amsterdam shores, the French captain told Levy and the other Jews that they did not have enough money or personal property to pay for their passage, and he would not let them go until the debt was paid to his satisfaction. Asser, again using his business sense, negotiated an auction with some of the citizens in the tiny Dutch outpost to sell off their possessions to help raise enough money to satisfy their debt. The auction brought some money to the passengers, and to Asser's astonishment, the buyers, in an uncharacteristic mood of Christian charity, wound up giving back most of these items to their original Jewish owners, believing that the new arrivals would need them if they were to settle in New Amsterdam.

However, the money paid to Captain de la Motthe was insufficient for the passage, and he became increasingly impatient. Thankfully, a local New Amsterdam inhabitant came to the rescue of the small group. He had found a loophole in the law that permitted the hijacked Jews to pay off their debt, with interest to the sailors of the French ship, who legally had the right to collect their monies. The crew agreed to the arrangements, and finally Asser and the little band of refugees were released to begin the next chapter in their lives in New Amsterdam. When Levy and the others were informed that they were free, they raised their hands to the heavens and thanked God for leading them to their new home.

When Asser Levy and the other Jews arrived in New Amsterdam, what awaited them was a colony under the control of iron-fisted, autocratic, and bigoted Peter Stuyvesant. Before his arrival here, drinking was rampant, there was open knife fighting in the streets, white inhabitants were fornicating with the local natives, and a sense of general lawlessness prevailed. New Amsterdam was reminiscent of "Dodge City" in the old West. Stuyvesant proceeded to lay down the law. One of the provisos was that no churches, except those belonging to the Dutch Reform Church, would be tolerated.

This was a problem of course for Asser and his fellow Jews since their Jewish High Holy Day of Rosh Hashanah was approaching and the tiny band had no place to worship. Luckily, an empathetic member of the Dutch community allowed Asser Levy and the other Jewish men and older boys to meet secretly in his windmill, on what is now Stone Street, to conduct services. This was the beginning of the Shearith Israel (Remnants of Israel) Congregation, the oldest Jewish congregation in the New World.

When the Jews arrived, Stuyvesant faced a new problem. He vowed that he would not allow the people of the Jewish nation to "infest" New Amsterdam. So he decided to petition the Dutch West India Company to have these "heathens" removed from the colony. What Stuyvesant failed to realize was that many of the stockholders in the Company were themselves Jewish. Seven months later, when a ship arrived from the Netherlands, it carried a letter from the Dutch West India Company, giving the Jews permission to stay. The letter also admonished Stuyvesant for his bigotry and reminded him that this was not a religious colony but one strictly set up for business purposes. Any person who could contribute to the development of New Amsterdam was welcome to stay.

So Asser and the others were allowed to stay in the town, but not without limitations. For example, the Jews could not own property, conduct certain types of businesses, carry a firearm, build a house of worship, or even be buried within the city limits. Also, they could not stand guard on the newly built wall that Stuyvesant had ordered constructed to cross the island of Manhattan from east to west. Stuyvesant's purpose in building the wall was to protect the inhabitants of his Dutch colony from the Native Americans, the wolves (Manhattan was a hilly, heavily forested area in 1654), and their dreaded enemy, the English, who happened to have colonies surrounding the tiny isolated colony at the tip of the island. Even though the Jewish people could not stand guard on the wall, Stuyvesant made them pay a tax for *not* standing guard. But Asser Levy would not accept these edicts. He wanted to be an equal member of the community by both contributing his fair share of taxes and by taking his turn on the wall to defend it. Asser again took matters in his own hands. He wrote to Dutch West India Company officials, stating his wishes that he and the other Jewish people be treated like everyone else in New Amsterdam. Eventually, due to Asser Levy's efforts, this edict was rescinded and the Jews took their rightful place on the wall with their fellow citizens.

Today, Shearith Israel is housed at a very different location, in a beautiful synagogue on Central Park West, just north of the famed Tavern on the Green Restaurant, and New York City boasts the largest Jewish population in the world outside of Israel. And to think, it all started with Asser Levy and his little band of exiles.

40,880 BULLETS

1776

It was July 9, 1776. The crowd of soldiers and civilians stood in silence, anticipating the reading of the most important document of their lives. They knew that Thomas Jefferson, Benjamin Franklin, and John Adams, three of the greatest minds of the day, had completed their work in Philadelphia, where the document was read on July 4, and it was now going to be their turn to hear it. At about 6:00 p.m. the American soldiers were ordered to gather at New York's Common. General Washington, in full dress uniform, rode up on his white steed. One of his aides was holding a rolled parchment in his hand. Other citizens of the city had gathered around the troops. After a brief word from the general, the aide began to read in a strong, calm voice, "When in the course of human events it becomes necessary for one people to dissolve the political bands which have connected them with another and to assume among them the powers of the earth, the separate and equal station to which the Laws of Nature and of Nature's God entitle them, a decent respect to the opinions of mankind requires that they declare the causes which impel them to the separation."

The New Yorkers knew that this day would come and they were ready. It was time to tear off the yoke of British tyranny and show the king that they were not going to take his mistreatment anymore. After all, they had been loyal British subjects who had fought for king and country, not second-class citizens. As soon as the Declaration was read, many members of the crowd sprang into action. They were going to rid themselves of British rule once and for all, and what better way to start than by pulling down this symbol of their hated monarch, the statue of King George?

They were determined to rid themselves of the British Empire, which felt the American colonies should pay for the privilege of being protected from the French by the British government after the French and Indian War. The same British government that instituted the 1765 Stamp Tax that was put on all paper transactions in the American colonies. Of course when the Americans decided to tar and feather the tax collectors as a form of protest, the king and British Parliament got wind of it, and upon the insistence of the colonists, the king agreed to repeal the hated act, but not without putting up a statue of himself in downtown New York (to the tune of 1,000 pounds) complete with a royal fence around it to remind the colonists of how kind he was to listen to their complaints and repeal the act. The colonists were okay with this for a while, but then a new series of taxes were instituted on the colonists, and the more the Americans protested the tighter the king's restrictions became. The Americans were outraged that even after they had demonstrated their loyalty to the king by erecting a statue in his honor, he had betrayed them with new taxes and edicts.

People were aching for a revolution. Battles raged in Lexington, Concord, and Bunker Hill. Then Boston was taken hostage by the British. George Washington, commander in chief, decided New York City was where Americans were going to make their stand.

The general arrived in the city in the spring of 1776. By the time the Declaration of Independence was read on July 9, 1776, their seething anger erupted. Since the king was three thousand miles away and could not be attacked personally, the only recourse that they had was to destroy his likeness in a symbolic gesture of disgust.

"Impeach the king! Down with tyranny! Tar and feather him!" shouted the crowd as they approached the king on his equestrian landmark, which stood regally on its pedestal in the center of Bowling Green Park, the oldest park in New York City. The crowd of colonists made its way down Broadway. When they reached the park, they slowly circled the great statue, surveying the situation. Suddenly a group of about forty men led by Captain Oliver Brown sprang forward. They threw long ropes over the statue and tied them in large knots in order to get a better grip. Then, seething with anger, they began to pull with all their might. The rest of the crowd backed away, waiting in anticipation for what would happen next. The giant statue began to rock back and forth on its base. All of a sudden, there was a thunderous crash, and the crowd cheered wildly. The "king" was dead.

But that wasn't enough. Others armed with crowbars and axes began to dismember the statue. They severed the head from the body and hacked off the wreath and nose. They passed the head around from man to man until it was dropped and began to roll unceremoniously down Broadway, where it was retrieved by members of the angry mob. The tail of the horse was then yanked off. Other parts of both man and horse were smashed by the crowd, which had now worked itself into frenzy. Next, a partially drunken mob, led by the patriot Isaac Sears, raced to the fence that surrounded the park. Sears and the others systematically sawed off the king's crowns on each of the thick supporting fence sections. They threw the crowns into a pile with other pieces from the statue while members of the mob played "The Rogue's March," normally associated with the tarring and feathering of a tortured victim. Then the men gathered up the debris, dragged it off, and shipped it to other colonial outposts. Part of the king's dismembered body found its way to Litchfield, Connecticut, a burgeoning American military depot. The metal from the king's statue was melted and transformed into bullets (40,880, to be precise), and these bullets were fired against the British.

The next day, General Washington called for Captain Brown and questioned him regarding the events of the previous evening. Brown was not sure whether he would be punished for his actions and those of his men. Washington may or may not have been an actual witness to the statue's demise, but it still occurred under his watch. After several minutes Brown had his answer. The general, all six feet three inches of him, a giant of a man, rose to his feet and pronounced, "The general doubts not that the persons who pulled down and mutilated the statue were actuated by zeal in the public cause, yet it has so much the appearance of riot and want of order in the army that he disproves the manner and directs that in the future these things shall be avoided by the soldiery and left to be executed by proper authority." Washington told Brown to get back to his duties and the incident was not mentioned again.

The Patriots' actions started the battle for control of New York City between the Americans and the British. Although the city remained in British hands for most of the American Revolution, the citizens fought for their independence and were able to claim victory when the British were finally evacuated from New York City in 1783.

NEW YORKERS UPSET ABOUT LIFE ON THE MOON

1835

It had been a hot, muggy summer. New Yorkers were busy hurrying off to work. The newspaper boys who sold papers for the *New York Sun* (the most widely read newspaper in the city at the time) were hustling their papers at a penny a pop to be able to eat that night.

No one knew on that Friday morning, August 21, 1835, that a single sentence in the *Sun* under the heading "Celestial Discoveries" would change history. That sentence read, "We have just learnt from an eminent publisher in this city that Sir John Herschel, at the Cape of Good Hope, has made some astronomical discoveries of the most wonderful description, by means of an immense telescope of an entirely new principle."

Four days later, the *Sun* began the publication of a "series of articles" written by Sir John Herschel called "Great Astronomical Discoveries." These "journal entries" described in detail that life had been discovered on the moon. Now we are not talking tiny little atoms, but a whole cavalcade of life, from water birds to unicorns to beavers that walked upright on two legs and carried their young in their arms to four-foot-tall creatures with wings dubbed "man-bats," or its Latin name, *Vespertilio-homo,* that conversed, built temples made of polished sapphire and gold, and fornicated in public.

The papers couldn't sell fast enough. Thousands of newspaper boys lined up from dawn to midnight outside the *New York Sun*'s office to hopefully get jobs delivering these papers to the hungry masses waiting for the latest updates. Everyone was talking about it . . . from the rich to the poor, from New York to Great Britain, Italy, Germany, and France. The question on everyone's lips was, "Have you heard the news of the man in the Moon?"

Meanwhile, inside the *Sun* building located at the corner of Spruce and Nassau, thirty-four-year-old Richard Adam Locke, editor of the *New York Sun*, sat at his office desk in amazement. Locke was one of America's first court reporters and had a very credible reputation. But a few weeks prior, Locke was leafing through an old volume of *The Edinburgh New Philosophical Journal* and came upon an article written by respected scientists called, "The Moon and its inhabitants." He thought it nonsense. But at the time, people were waiting for the arrival of Halley's Comet, which only comes every seventy-five to seventy-six years and was due to streak across the skies of America. People's minds were spaceward. A flash of brilliance came. He approached his publisher, Benjamin Day, and said he wanted to write a moon series. He asked for an astronomical fee of $500 for the entire series, the equivalent of a year's salary. Day agreed. Locke then mixed his passion for astronomy with his fabulous writing abilities to produce an 11,000-word narrative detailed with scientific description over a period of ten days. The thing was he never thought people would believe it was real. But they did, and it became the biggest hoax of the century. Whether Day knew it was real or not is not certain; what is certain is that it sold papers, and lots of them.

Locke's story convinced readers that the observation of these creatures was possible with a new device that combined the powers of the hydro-oxygen microscope (a real microscope) with the telescope, providing astronomers with a view of the moon never before seen.

But he went one step further. He credited the discovery of these creatures to John Herschel, who was the world's leading astronomer at the time (his dad, William Herschel, discovered Uranus). The paper read, "For there in the red-hilled valley, Sir John Herschel first beheld lunar animals. They could clearly make out a heard of large brown quadrupeds; with their curved horns, humped shoulders, and shaggy fur, the animals closely resembled earthly bison, although they possessed a 'fleshy appendage' over their eyes, like a hairy veil, which Sir John quickly identified as a 'providential contrivance' to protect the eyes from the moon's extremes of light and darkness." Then it went on in detail to describe other such discoveries, including the area Sir John named the region of the "Valley of the Unicorn."

Locke said that Herschel's entire account of the new moon findings had been published in the "Edinburgh Journal of Science," which made it sound credible.

Herschel of course had no idea that any of this was going on because he was working at the Cape of Good Hope, far away from New York City. He had toyed with the idea of life on the moon but had never seen anything outside of the lunar seas. By the time any newspaper would reach him via sailing ships, the hoax would long be over.

In the meantime, the *New York Sun* was raking in the dough. At first it was just a series of articles, running daily, each about four columns long, but they became so popular that on August 29, the *Sun* had to put out a pamphlet called "A Complete Account of the Late Discoveries in the Moon." It was quickly put together and sold for twelve and a half cents a copy. But people wanted more: They began to demand to see pictures of these creatures. So Locke headed down to Wall Street and found what he reported in the paper as the most "talented lithographic artist in the city." He found Mr. Baker of Norris and Baker. Within twenty-four hours of the *Sun* reporting the discovery of these man-bats, lithograph drawings were produced and sold at a whopping twenty-five cents a pop under the name "Lunar Animals and Other Objects."

P. T. Barnum, the man who brought the circus to town at the time and introduced New Yorkers to bizarre creatures, was deeply impressed. He later wrote, "They sold no less than $25,000 worth of moon-hoax paraphernalia." Considering there were only 250,000 people at the time in New York, those were huge numbers. Day said later it was sixty thousand sold (today that would be about a million copies). What was even more amazing was the turnaround. The *Sun* had been founded just two years earlier by Day as a way to advertise his printing shop; this little moon hoax now made him the proud owner of the most widely read newspaper in the world!

Locke had no idea how big this idea of his had gotten. He was just busy pumping out the details. One day, however, he went into the street shortly after the paper came out to hear people's reaction. He was shocked. He heard an elderly gentleman dressed in a "fine broadcloth Quaker suit" say that he himself had seen the great tele-scope described in the *Sun* articles. Another man claimed to own a copy of the supplement to the *Edinburgh Journal of Science* from which the *Sun* had been publishing excerpts, and so far he had found no errors or lapses in the newspaper's reprint. Locke was amazed; the people themselves were perpetuating the hoax.

Other papers, such as the *Evening Post,* that were copying the story due to public demand said they were reporting it because it was "very important if true, and if not true, the reader will still be obliged to confess that it is very ingenious." Some praised the penny paper; other larger papers like the *Enquirer* looked down on the "penny trash."

The lunar discoveries made their final appearance in the *Sun* on Monday, August 31. The final article explained that after a full day of viewing man-bats Herschel went to bed early, only to be awoken a few hours later by shouts that the observatory where the telescope was housed was on fire. By the time the fire was put out, the reflectors were fused together into "useless clumps of metal." Supposedly masonry workers and carpenters were summoned to Cape Town, and within a week the telescope was working again, but unfortunately the moon was invisible and John Herschel was then looking at other planets. They looked again in March and observed some more life, but the *Sun* said the rest of the journal was just mathematical equations and would not be of interest to the reader.

The day after the series ended, a rival editor from the *Herald*, James Gordon Bennett, wrote a piece called "The Astronomical Hoax Explained" and said Locke was the genius behind the piece but made some serious blunders. In an open public letter Locke politely and skillfully denied that he had "made those discoveries." Bennett persisted, being careful not to turn the public against him. Locke said little. The *Sun* denied it.

Locke became depressed and one night in a drunken stupor admitted to a fellow reporter who wanted to republish the piece that he wrote it. The reporter wrote the scoop. The *Sun* denied it. The moon series in two weeks made its way into pop culture.

As for Locke, he left the *Sun* and went on to edit two other major dailies. On October 3, 1836, in one of his papers' bylines, Locke identified himself for the first time publicly as the hoax's creator but gave no explanation. Five years later, on May 16, 1840, in the *New World* newspaper, he revealed the whole truth, that he wrote it because religious astronomers of his day professed belief in the existence of life on the moon, so he wanted to give the world what they wanted to believe in, life on the moon. It was intended as a satire, not a hoax.

For two more decades people still believed the moon series to be gospel. The *Sun*'s circulation never went down, and New Yorkers have always admitted and loved the ingenuity of the hoax.

Even though Locke went on to write many fantastic things, he would forever be known as "the man on the moon," the man who had created the most successful hoax in the history of American journalism. It was a title he grew to detest.

THE SWEDISH NIGHTINGALE

1850

It was September 11, 1850. A plain-looking, slightly plump twenty-nine-year-old woman anxiously waited in the wings behind the stage of Castle Garden at the tip of Manhattan Island, listening for her musical cue. Her hair was plain and straight, her nose broad. She was dressed in a modest plain white silk dress and wore no jewelry, which was a sharp contrast to those in attendance awaiting her arrival. The audience was made up of the most notable people in New York City, including the mayor, prominent merchants, and members of the city's most elite families. They were decked out in their finest clothes and jewels. Many of the women had coiffed their hair to emulate the style worn by the lady who was about to grace them with her presence.

The orchestra leader raised his baton, a few chords of music sounded, and the massive velvet stage curtain parted. The audience was somewhat surprised at her appearance, considering that she was the toast of the European stage and had been showered with gifts from the royals all over the continent. They expected elegance, jewels, and the finest apparel. Instead they saw a young woman who stood silently on the stage for a few moments and did not even look directly at them. The atmosphere was tense. Then her eyes grew moist as the crowd burst into wild cheering and applauding. A modest and pure expression covered her rounded face, making it seem childlike, glistening with serenity. The orchestra began to play. As the sound of music filled the room, the young woman lifted her gaze toward the audience and began to sing. The audience was mesmerized.

Jenny Lind, "the Swedish Nightingale," had come to New York. When she stood on the stage of the five-thousand-seat amphitheater, no one could have imagined that this Swedish-speaking young woman, who was also fluent in German, while struggling with English, would set the city and the country ablaze with her performances. But New Yorkers were ready to embrace her. They had been prepared for the event by the great impresario P. T. Barnum. Barnum had spent months prepping the media and Americans for Jenny's arrival in New York and her planned grand concert tour of the United States. He had billed the event as the "most spectacular demonstration of vocal quality ever seen in the world." Because of all the hype and hoopla created by Barnum, the tickets for this September 11 performance had to be sold at auction. The Castle Garden amphitheater, which had previously been a fort built in 1811 to stave off a potential British attack on New York City, had a capacity of five thousand seats. Some tickets wound up costing $650 for a normal $5 seat. (Remember, this was 1850, so in today's equivalent dollars, it was $10,000 per ticket!)

Not bad for someone who was only on the planet for thirty years. Lind was born in Sweden in 1820. She spent her early years touring Europe, where she met and performed with some of the greatest composers in history. Her voice outshined her looks, so even though she was plain looking, she attracted many suitors. Reportedly the great writer Hans Christian Andersen had expressed love and intentions toward Jenny, even though he was married. Jenny was the inspiration for three of his most famous fairy tales: "The Ugly Duckling," "The Angel," and "The Nightingale," the latter of which gave her the nickname the Swedish Nightingale. The great classic composer Felix Mendelssohn also was smitten with Jenny's charms.

The incomparable Ms. Lind, however, was more than just a great voice; she was a good businesswoman, too. Prior to coming to America, she had negotiated with Barnum to deposit $187,000 in a London bank as "up front" money and guarantee for her concert tour. In one case he had a hotel owner pay $1,000 a night for the "privilege" of hosting Jenny Lind. In another instance, Barnum approached a Philadelphia minister to lend him $5,000. He persuaded the minister that Lind, with her wholesomeness, would be an excellent influence on the morals of American society, and the minister agreed. Finally, the impresario himself had to mortgage all his commercial and residential properties to secure the funds he needed to come up with the balance. Barnum then sent the money to the London bank as Lind had requested.

In order to further promote Jenny Lind's six New York appearances and the rest of the concert tour, and to help defray some of the costs associated with them, Barnum and other entrepreneurs sold posters, porcelain pieces, cards, photographs, lamps, and even soap, all with Jenny's likeness on them. The investment paid off. For the New York concerts alone, Barnum grossed over $100,000 (in 1850 dollars), a figure unequalled either before or since for a concert.

Were the tickets worth these prices? Did Jenny Lind truly possess the voice of a nightingale, or was this just one of Mr. Barnum's theatrical ploys to make money? It did not take the audience very long to have its answer. Almost from the first bar of the aria, "Casta Diva" from the *Norma,* those assembled in the auditorium were enraptured with her voice. It was crystal clear and full of expression. Jenny Lind did not simply sing a song, but brought out its soul. Every note embodied what the composer meant to say with his music.

At the instant the diva finished singing her first song, the audience broke into thunderous applause. The crowd rose to its feet and continued the ovation for several minutes, not letting Miss Lind continue the concert. All the while the Nightingale quietly and shyly bowed in acknowledgement of the accolades. Finally, when the crowd returned to their seats, Jenny continued her performance both as a soloist and in duets with the most famed tenor of the day, Signor Belletti. Each time she sang, she received the cheers from the spectators. Never in New York City had a singer so captured an audience as Jenny Lind did on that September evening. When the performance finally drew to a close, the applause was tumultuous. The audience did not want her to leave the stage. Jenny simply remained silent with her arms across her chest, bowing in acceptance for the admiration shown by the crowd of New Yorkers. Finally, after what must have seemed like an eternity to Jenny, P. T. Barnum himself came on stage to say a few words about Jenny Lind's performance and about her generosity. Everyone who walked out of Castle Garden that night felt as if they had gotten what they had paid for and more.

Lind had been scheduled for one hundred fifty performances, but after ninety-three, she and Barnum parted ways. This was partly due to Barnum's driven personality and the "task master" approach he used on Jenny. It may also have been the influence of her accompanist, Otto Goldschmidt, with whom her relationship was ever growing. Goldschmidt, a former student of Mendelssohn, proposed to Jenny during the American tour. They were married in Massachusetts on February 5, 1852. After completing their tour, the couple went back to Europe and had three children. Overall, Jenny Lind's concert appearances under Barnum's management netted

$712,161.34 with just over a half million going to the showman and $208,675 to the singer.

But it was not all about money for Jenny Lind, as New Yorkers and other Americans found out. She donated her share of the proceeds from two of her concerts to twelve different New York City charitable organizations, with the lion's share going to the New York City Fire Department to help support widows and orphans. She also gave a friend $5,000 to purchase a new camera for his Chicago photography studio. The camera was later used to create Matthew Brady's images of Abraham Lincoln so that posterity had a way of remembering this great man. (She also sat for a photographic portrait for Brady himself in his New York City studio, prior to her leaving on her American tour.) In almost every town that she visited, Jenny Lind gave some share of her profits to the community. Many of these towns named streets in her honor, including McKeesport, Pennsylvania, and Easton, Massachusetts. An entire gold rush town in California was named Jennyland. To further honor her influence and generosity, a furniture manufacturer named a crib after her, a name it still bears today. When she returned to Europe, the praises and honors continued. An infirmary for sick children in London was named in her honor, her likeness was put on Sweden's fifty kronor banknote, and there was even a Jenny Lind locomotive.

Jenny Lind may have possessed the greatest voice the world has ever known, but unfortunately there is no way to ever really know, since she sang in the days before there were recordings. All that we do know for sure is that she was a rare talent whose performances moved audiences. She possessed not only a beautiful voice but also a warm, sincere, and generous nature. She received accolades wherever she went for both her singing and her charity. Jenny Lind was truly one of the greatest performers to have ever graced a stage.

THE TALL, UNATTRACTIVE MAN

1860

On the cold wintry evening of February 27, 1860, Abraham Lincoln stood on a train platform. He was a tall, unattractive man with a pock-marked face who entered New York City with no fanfare. His mission was to present himself as a viable candidate for the presidency of the United States. He knew that one of his biggest challenges was to make a positive impression on the New York press. He was a modest and humble man, and up until this point in his life he had experienced numerous failures. But he refused to give up. He felt that he possessed a keen understanding of human nature, and a compassion for the common man, traits he believed would come through when he spoke.

Abraham Lincoln was a frontier lawyer from the great undeveloped state of Illinois, and on this February evening, he was going to introduce himself to the people of the country at one of their most illustrious venues, the Great Hall of Cooper Union in New York City. Originally, Lincoln was invited by Mr. James Briggs to give a lecture, Lincoln believed, on the question of slavery, at Plymouth

Church in Brooklyn and was offered $200 for his time. It was also suggested that, since he was coming east, perhaps he could also speak in New York City. That's when the wheels in Lincoln's head began to turn. In 1856 he had run as the Republican Party's vice-presidential candidate and his party lost the national election. Why not seek the party's nomination for the highest office in the land in the upcoming election? Why not take this opportunity to turn this speaking engagement into a political speech? Little did he realize, at the time, that this was exactly what one faction of the Republican Party was counting on. Lincoln wrote back to Briggs with his proposal to speak in February at both venues and received the following response: "You may lecture the time you mention, and will pay you $200. I think they (Young Republicans) will arrange for a lecture in New York, also, and will pay you $200 for that, with your consent. Thus you may kill two birds with one stone."

The *New York Tribune,* who supported the idea of a Lincoln candidacy, ran the following statement: "The distinguishing characteristics of his political addresses are clearness and candor of statement, a chivalrous courtesy to opponents, and a broad, genial humor. Let us crowd the Cooper Institute to hear him Monday night."

As the audience descended the stairs to the basement of Cooper Union and into the confines of the Great Hall, they were talking about this stranger from the west whom they were about to hear. What does he look like? What does he sound like? What will be his message? When the crowd of fifteen hundred finally entered the auditorium, the guest speakers of the evening were on the stage. The first two gentlemen were Senators Frank P. Blair of Missouri and Cassius M. Clay of Kentucky, both known for their antislavery rhetoric. Lincoln sat quietly, fidgeting slightly, while waiting for his turn to speak. He was surveying the members of the audience, trying to read their faces and getting a sense of their moods. Lincoln was then introduced by the moderator. He rose slowly to his feet to take his turn at the podium. For the first time, the spectators got a good look at "the man from Illinois." His initial appearance seems to have taken people aback. An eyewitness that evening said, "When Lincoln rose to speak, I was greatly disappointed. He was tall, tall, oh, how tall! and so angular and awkward that I had, for an instant, a feeling of pity for so ungainly a man." However, once Lincoln warmed up, "his face lighted up as with an inward fire; the whole man was transfigured. I forgot his clothes, his personal appearance, and his personal peculiarities. Presently forgetting myself, I was on my feet like the rest, yelling like a wild Indian, cheering this wonderful man." The speech mesmerized the audience and helped Lincoln gain strong favor among the William Seward supporters who had initially preferred the New York governor as the Republican nominee for the presidency. A New York writer wrote, "No man ever before made such an impression on his first appeal to a New York audience."

Abraham Lincoln has been described in a myriad of ways, often contrasting his awkward physical appearance with the positive emotional persona he exhibited. Lincoln was characterized as a thin, narrow-shouldered, muscular man, standing six feet three and one half inches, and weighing about one hundred sixty pounds. He was indifferent to clothes, his unmanageable black hair was turning gray, and his small, sad, sunken gray eyes had dark rings below. Clean-shaven about the mouth but deeply bearded elsewhere, Lincoln had prominent ears, nose, and Adam's apple. His deeply lined face was careworn but filled with human sympathies. He was a man of simplicity and unpretentiousness. Another comment came from noted poet Walt Whitman, who said, "Though Lincoln's visage lacks technical beauty, it furnishes an artist a rare study, a feast, and fascination." The *New York Times* reported that, "Lincoln resembles George Washington, having great calmness of temper, great firmness of purpose, supreme moral principle, and intense patriotism." Lincoln even considered himself "the people's attorney, not their ruler."

Now, in the Great Hall at Cooper Union, there stood a man to be admired for his drive to never give up. Throughout his life he suffered many hardships, both personal and professional, including many political defeats, the death of his first love, and the loss of two of his adored sons. "The Great Emancipator" himself suffered from some type of ailment such as Marfan's Syndrome or a rare genetic disease (doctors are still debating the issue), which accounted for his awkward physical appearance. Even with all these setbacks, Lincoln preserved and maintained a good sense of humor. In fact, when Mary Todd Lincoln, who constantly berated her husband, asked a group of photographers, "Why are you taking pictures of the President? He is the ugliest man on the face of the earth," Lincoln's retort, after Mary exited the room of course, was, "Gentlemen, if I had another face, would I wear this one?"

That cold day in February of 1860, Lincoln's carefully crafted speech concentrated on the views of thirty-nine signers of the Constitution on the issue of slavery and the importance of preserving the Union. Lincoln noted, "That at least twenty-one of them, a majority, believed Congress should control slavery in the territories, not allow it to expand. Thus, the Republican stance of the time was not revolutionary, but similar to the Founding Fathers, and should not alarm Southerners." Then Lincoln went on to give the reason that the Republicans need to take the position that he espoused; the position that preserving the Union was the *most* important thing. With passion he implored them, "It is exceedingly desirable that all parts of this great Confederacy [he meant the United States] shall be at peace, and in harmony, one with another. Let us Republicans do our part to have it so." Lincoln concluded his remarks with words that have become part of the legacy of greatness that this tall, unattractive man left us. "Neither let us be slandered from our duty by false accusations against us, nor frightened from it by menaces of destruction to the Government nor of dungeons to ourselves. *Let us have faith that right makes might, and in that faith, let us, to the end, dare to do our duty as we understand it."*

Obviously, greatness cannot be judged on looks alone. It was the heart, soul, and passion of Lincoln's speech that moved the people in the audience on that day, and would continue to move them for several years to come. When Lincoln had finished, the audience was in awe. The Republicans had found their candidate, and the rest is history!

THE SECRET SUBWAY

1870

On the early morning of February 26, 1870, the press and assorted dignitaries were treated to a "Fashionable Reception held in the Bowels of the Earth!" as the *New York Herald* proclaimed.

There, under the crowded streets of Broadway, hundreds of invited guests gathered in a 120-foot gorgeous waiting room that looked more like an elegant apartment, complete with grand piano, a goldfish-stocked fountain, chandeliers, and lavish paintings. A warm glow from bright lamps bathed the underground lobby.

When everyone's curiosity was at its peak, a man jumped to the podium and announced, "We propose to operate a subway all the way to Central Park, about five miles in all. When it's finished we should be able to carry twenty thousand passengers a day at speeds up to a mile a minute. This means the end of street dust." Reporters jotted down notes, dignitaries applauded, and with that the crowd was led to view the first ever of its kind, a subway. Not just any subway, but a pneumatic subway that was powered by a huge fan that moved people in a car through a tube by means of compressed air. For the small price of a quarter, curious onlookers got a ride in the twenty-two-seat spacious subway car with nice cushiony seats. It was an instant winner.

A man stood back smiling. Now all he had to do was get financial backing and government approval . . . because you see the catch was, this subway was built without any government officials or New Yorkers having the slightest clue.

Who was the mastermind of this secret plot? He was none other than Alfred Ely Beach, a man comfortable with grand ideas. As a co-publisher of the *New York Sun,* he was also a patent attorney and inventor, who had already surprised the world with this cable railway and the world's first practical typewriter, which won him a gold medal at the Crystal Palace Exposition in 1853.

So why then did he have to build a secret subway? Beach saw a problem: too many yelling wagon drivers, neighing horses, and people all squashed together at the corners of Broadway and Chambers. He knew he either had to divert traffic above or below ground. He didn't like the idea of unsightly elevated trains so he decided to go subterrain.

Since readily available gas and electric cars weren't possible yet, he looked at an existing idea, one that the post offices in England were using: pneumatic power.

Once he had the idea, he built a small-scale prototype and unveiled it three years earlier at the American Institute Fair, which was held at the Fourteenth Street Armory. His working model was a wooden tube shell, one and a half inches thick, made up of fifteen layers of laminated veneer and joined together with cement. The tube was six feet in diameter and one hundred feet in length. It hung aboveground "suspended from the wall, and ran from galley to galley, a distance of one hundred and seven feet."

The motor power was a ten-foot, eight-blade propeller fan making two hundred revolutions per minute. That burst of air would shoot the inner car with the people in it quietly through the tube. For display purposes it ran between Fourteenth and Fifteenth Streets in mere seconds. Once at the end of the tube, the fan was put in reverse and the people were sucked back.

His invention was a sensation. In his book he writes, "The proposed cost would not exceed $100 (per foot) or $500,000 per mile, much below the cost of an underground steam-run railroad."

Excited, he went back to the drawing board to create a tool that could dig a tunnel under the streets of Broadway, so he could build a real functional subway. Like any good genius, he invented a hydraulic tunnel driller that could bore through seventeen inches of earth wall with each press of the lever, complete with a shield to protect the workers in case of cave-ins. The machine could move left and right, up and down.

He was ready but the politicos weren't—namely, Tammany Hall, a Democratic political machine, and its head honcho, Boss Tweed. Tweed was the most corrupt and powerful politician of his time whose grubby greased hands dug deep into everyone's pie. There was no way Tweed was going to let this subway be built, unless it was blowing major money into his pocket through the intimidation of political blackmail and kickbacks.

The choices? Quit, give into blackmail, or do it on the sneak? Beach chose to be a sly fox, an extremely dangerous and costly choice, especially with the eyes and ears of City Hall at every turn. It would require great stealth and a cover story. Beach pretended he was working on a mail system and obtained a permit for such.

Since he couldn't operate openly, he had to fund the subway largely with his own money, to the tune of $350,000. He convinced some close associates, however, that if he built something so beautiful and efficient that when the final product was revealed, Tweed publicly would have no option but to allow the subway to stay, lest he'd look bad in the eyes of the public. His associates agreed and helped him with the secret project.

So Beach rented the basement of Devlin's clothing Store at Murray Street and Broadway, right across the street from Tweed's office. In 1868 he hired his twenty-one-year-old son, Fred, to act as foreman. Fred and his secret gang would haul out dirt and hide it behind the clothing store.

Over the next fifty-eight nights they ran into some construction obstacles. Some men quit for fear of cave-ins from the horses running above; some quit because the claustrophobia got to them. At one point while digging, they literally hit a brick wall, a fortress from bygone days. Beach told the men to remove the wall, "stone by stone!" Many were scared and quit; others continued drilling. Each night the brave workers silently removed dirt and stone in wagons whose wheels had been specially made to be quiet. "Gangs of men slipped in and out of the tunnel like thieves," wrote Robert Daley later in *The World Beneath the City*.

Finally the tube was set and a single car, which fitted tightly into the pneumatic nine-foot tube, was set. The workers nicknamed the project "The Western Tornado" because of its motor, and it ran from Warren Street to Murray Street. A bell at the other end would ring, and the car was then sucked back to the start at ten miles an hour. This was the real working deal.

Then came the big reveal. Needless to say, Tweed and his cronies were not happy campers. But Tweed realized he had a worthy opponent, a man who was not afraid to defy him and who could seriously cut into his underhanded profits.

Tweed called Beach to his office and tried to "persuade him" to hand over or quit his project. But Beach had the public on his side. The subway was not only a proven moneymaker but also an improvement to the city. "I will go before the legislature in Albany," Beach protested.

The New York State Senate and State Assembly gave their thumbs-up, and his $5 million plan all to be raised with private funding was approved. Instead of fighting Beach, Tweed came up with an underhanded counterattack and leaned on his political partners to support him. Tweed proposed an elevated train line costing $80 million of taxpayers' money, which was also approved. The final say would lie in the hands of Governor John T. Hoffman, a good friend of Tweed's, who would benefit nicely from Tweed's transportation method. Tweed's was approved, and Beach's ultimately denied.

Beach, undeterred, launched a publicity campaign, and the unanimous vote on the street was for the pneumatic train. The bill came up again. Tweed, who had been losing some ground as man in command, still put pressure on people, and Beach lost again, but this time by only one vote.

A year later, Tweed's corrupt ring was exposed, and the Beach Transit bill was passed by Governor Dix, but at a price: Beach was emotionally, physically, and financially drained, and to top it off, the public had lost interest in the novelty train.

In addition, Beach wound up alienating super landlord, John Astor, who was afraid the subway might weaken the foundation of his prize property, Trinity Church, the tallest building in Manhattan at the time.

Beach now had a bittersweet victory. He now had the approval but no funds. With no interest or investors, Dix withdrew the charter for the subway.

The subway died a quiet death, until February 1912, when a group of workers digging for what they believed to be the first ever subway system found the Beach tunnel and lobby in all its glory with the railroad car still on its tracks.

They decided to honor Beach's engineering achievement, and to this day a plaque in his honor stands on the wall of the BMT subway line at City Hall Station, a few feet from where the whole thing started.

MADAM PRESIDENT

1872

An attractive young woman with beautifully coiffed hair, wearing a meticulously designed silk dress and matching hat, rose to speak at the podium. With passion in her eyes and a whimsical smile on her face, she stood before an admiring crowd of fifteen hundred rousing, cheering supporters at the Apollo Hall in New York City. With a wave of her hand, she quieted the audience and then spoke the words that they had come to hear her say, "I accept the nomination as a candidate for the presidency." The date was May 10, 1872, and Victoria Woodhull, spiritualist, owner of *The Woodhull/Claflin Weekly,* first woman to address Congress, owner of a female brokerage firm, and suffragette, made the startling announcement of her candidacy, which, to paraphrase the old television show *Star Trek,* would take her where no woman in America had gone before.

This was a woman filled with vibrant controversy. Victoria Woodhull lived in an era when women could only imagine what it would be like to have the right to vote. In 1872 equal pay for equal work was the farthest thing from women's minds. It was a time of hypocrisy when people preached strict morality but did just as they pleased, in business and in bed. Often, details of these indiscretions were covered up, distorted, or written strictly from the male viewpoint, even many years after they occurred.

The illustrious Ms. Woodhull was a perfect example of this. One of the things that she did as the publisher of her newspaper was to expose the noted Brooklyn preacher, Henry Ward Beecher, as an adulterer. "Our heroine" and the preacher may have had an amorous relationship themselves, and he spurned her. This might have been the reason that Victoria began her mudslinging campaign against him. It was a vendetta in a time when women had little recourse. You know the old adage, "Hell hath no fury like a woman scorned." Victoria's efforts in exposing Beecher eventually led to a trial at his own church on the charge of adultery. However, being a woman, she had little chance of coming out on top in this battle, and eventually she lost almost everything. Did she take this course of action because she believed that she was right, or did she do it simply because her vanity and ego were hurt? You decide.

But let's go back to that time when one woman took an unprecedented step, not only in talking about voting rights but also in actually running for President of the United States in order to give her rhetoric real clout. In March 1870, Victoria Claflin Woodhull first announced her intention to run for the Presidency of the United States in the 1872 election by penning a letter to the *New York Herald* newspaper. In it she made the following points: "As I happen to be the most prominent representative of the only unrepresented class in the republic, and perhaps the most practical exponent of the principles of equality, I request the favor of being permitted to address the public through the *Herald.* While others of my sex devoted themselves to a crusade against the laws that shackle the women of the country, I asserted my individual independence; while others prayed for the good time coming,

I worked for it; while others argued the equality of woman with man, I proved it by successfully engaging in business; while others sought to show that there was no valid reason why women should be treated, socially and politically, as inferior to man, I boldly entered the arena of politics and business and exercised the rights I already possessed. I therefore claim the right to speak for the unenfranchised women of the country, and believing as I do that the prejudices which still exist in the popular mind against women in public life will soon disappear, I now announce myself as a candidate for the Presidency." Amazingly, the *Herald* not only printed her letter but also published a favorable editorial commending her as "the lady broker" who had the financial credentials, courage, and determination to run for office.

A little less than a year later, in February 1871, Victoria Woodhull was given the "privilege" of addressing Congress on the issue of women's rights, something that Susan B. Anthony and other suffragettes had been unable to do. (Maybe it had something to do with her good looks, but who's to say?) On this unprecedented occasion, Victoria reiterated her reasons for her candidacy for the presidency and answered her critics, who believed that she was just an ambitious female who was out for her own glory. "Because I have taken this bold and positive position; because I have advocated radical political action; because I have announced a new party (Equal Rights Party) and myself as a candidate for the next presidency, I am charged with being influenced by an unwarrantable ambition. Though this is scarcely the place for the introduction of a privileged question, I will, however, take this occasion to, once and for all time, state I have no personal ambition whatever. All that I have done, I did because I believed the interests of humanity would be advanced thereby. Had I been ambitious to become the next President, I should have proceeded very differently to accomplish this. I did announce myself as a candidate, and this simple fact has done a great work in compelling people to ask; and why not? This service that I have rendered women at the expense of my ambition I might have had, which is apparent if the matter be but candidly considered."

As Victoria stood in Apollo Hall on that spring day in 1872, she accepted the honor of being the standard bearer of the Equal Rights Party, which she had formed. Her supporters, who included suffragists, peace and temperance advocates, and spiritualists, embraced the platform that she put forth. Like everything that she did, Victoria was way ahead of her time in the proposals for her party: women's right to vote, work and love freely; nationalization of land; cost-based pricing to reduce excessive profits; a fairer division of earnings between capital and labor; the elimination of exorbitant interest rates; and free speech and a free press. Immediately after her nomination, Woodhull used her good business sense to establish strategies for her campaign. In another of her unprecedented moves, she selected as a running mate a black man, the brilliant and outspoken abolitionist Frederick Douglass (he may have not actually accepted the nomination), and laid out plans for their public speaking tours.

After the formal nomination, Victoria began to ration money that was to be used to fund her campaign from money that had been allocated from her early days in New York City, where she ran spiritualist sessions with her sister, the attractive Tennie C. Claflin. Little known to the public was most of the funds raised came from the generous advice of a newly widowed "tipster," none other than Cornelius Vanderbilt. Vanderbilt, who had recently lost his wife, was caught under Tennie's alluring spell, and his information and tips (today known as "insider trading") allowed Victoria and her sister to accumulate, with interest, $250,000 (today's equivalent of over $2.5 million).

Victoria Woodhull and Frederick Douglass's campaign pitted them against the two major candidates (both WASP males), the incumbent and highly popular Ulysses S. Grant and Horace Greeley ("Go west, young man, go west"), publisher of the *New York Tribune*. When the voting was all over, no surprise, Woodhull and Douglass didn't win! In fact, they only received about two thousand popular votes nationwide. But they planted a seed.

Women in the United States did not get the right to vote in national elections until 1920 under the Nineteenth Amendment. Since then, several women have run presidential campaigns, but usually only to focus on one specific issue. Only recently have women gained recognition as viable candidates for the major parties. How would Victoria have felt about Margaret Chase Smith's, Elizabeth Dole's, Shirley Chisholm's, and Bella Abzug's runs for the highest office in the land? Would she have rooted for Hillary Clinton to get her party's nomination, and perhaps have chosen Barack Obama as her vice president (shades of 1872)? Maybe someday Victoria's dream will come true and the United States will have a woman president. But until then, all we can do is remember that Victoria Claflin Woodhull's stance on women's rights and her bold move to express her ideas by running for the presidency started it all.

CLEOPATRA'S NEEDLE

1881

The sixty-nine-foot-tall object laid alongside the Ninety-sixth Street pier on the west side of Manhattan. It had to be moved almost a half mile across the city and into hilly Central Park. But what was this thing and how exactly were they going to move it? The object was an Egyptian obelisk, a stone pillar, built as a monument, that has a square base and sides that taper, like a pyramid, toward a pointed top. The plan was to construct a special train for the purpose, but the engineers soon realized that moving such a delicate structure this way would not work. So they had to devise another method to transport the massive two hundred twenty-four ton piece without damaging it. They decided to go back to the Egyptian drawing board and do what the ancient Egyptians had done: just roll it across the island. The structure was carefully lowered onto heavy boards using enormous ropes as guide wires. The boards rested on a system of cannon balls. When all was ready, the workmen began pushing and pulling the object forward at a snail's pace. Inch by inch the huge stone artifact began its journey.

The Obelisk, more fondly referred to as "Cleopatra's Needle," was actually moving toward its final resting place. As the stone pillar began moving across Manhattan, "obelisk fever" gripped New York. Curious onlookers lined the route, and every time even the slightest progress was made, they let out a cheer. Next came the souvenir hunters with their hammers and chisels. Armed guards had to be employed around the clock to protect the relic or there would be nothing left of it by the time it reached its final destination. One enterprising entrepreneur even set up a candy stand that traveled along with the obelisk and sold "Cleopatra dates" in special obelisk-shaped boxes. Upscale restaurants in the city offered a new drink, "the Obbylish," which was served with a needle-shaped swizzle stick.

What caused all this hype about a slab of granite? Well, there were a few reasons. First, the United States did not want to be shown up by its foreign allies. England had accepted a similar obelisk as a gift from the Khedive of Egypt in 1878, and France had accepted one in 1831. So when the Egyptian government offered one to the United States, various factions pushed hard to obtain the obelisk. "After all," one reporter stated, "it would be absurd for the people of my great city to be happy without having their own Egyptian obelisk!" Even President Rutherford B. Hayes, understanding the importance of public opinion, agreed that our country should have its own Egyptian relic.

The other reason the Khedive wanted to donate this massive structure to America was because of his desire to establish a business relationship based on the trade of Egyptian cotton. The end of the Civil War left the cotton industry in the South in a state of turmoil, and the Khedive saw this as an opportunity to gain political and economic favor for his generous gift.

However, there were numerous obstacles that America had to overcome. An artifact this large required an incredible feat to move due to its size and weight. Another obstacle came from its home port of Alexandria, whose residents disagreed with shipping any of Egypt's antiquities out of the country. If the obelisk was allowed to leave its homeland, the question of the cost to ship it to America became a major concern. Should it be underwritten by the government at the expense of the taxpayers, or should it be by private donation as a way for the rich to exploit their wealth?

The driving force behind the project to bring the obelisk to America was Henry Honeychurch Gorringe, an engineer who, while serving as a naval engineer in the Middle East, had first laid eyes on "Cleopatra's Needle." Immediately he began his quest to bring it to America. Gorringe was politically well connected with such financial backers as William H. Vanderbilt. Vanderbilt's $102,000 gift made it possible to get the project off the ground and to ship this monument overseas from Egypt to New York.

Vanderbilt, president of the New York Central Railroad, was the son of the famous robber baron, Commodore Cornelius Vanderbilt, one of the richest men in the world. Upon his father's death, William Vanderbilt became the primary beneficiary of this fabulous fortune. Later, he would take criticism for his comment, "Let the public be damned!" Paying for the obelisk was Vanderbilt's way of atoning for the comment. Once the obelisk was released by the Egyptian government, transporting it to America became a difficult and delicate operation. Gorringe had to open the side hull of the ship, roll the obelisk in, then seal up the opening and make it watertight. Because of the obelisk's weight and size, no other alternative was feasible.

Next, there was the issue of what to call the obelisk. It seemed it was a mistake to call it "Cleopatra's Needle," since the Queen of the Nile lived fifteen centuries after its erection, and her death occurred twelve years before its transport from its original site at Heliopolis to Alexandria. She probably would have never seen it or would have been aware of its existence.

A further controversy was the placement of the monument. Should it be at Columbus Circle or Union Square? It was finally agreed that the obelisk was to be placed on Greywache Knoll, a hill directly behind the Metropolitan Museum of Art and close to the Reservoir (later filled in by debris from the construction of Rockefeller Center in 1932 to create the Great Lawn of Central Park). This placement would be similar to its original waterside location at Heliopolis, on the Nile, or its later home at Alexandria, on the Mediterranean Sea.

Finally, the head of the Metropolitan Museum of Art and the commissioner of the "Obelisk Project" decided that time capsules should be placed within the base and the stairs, and they should contain representative objects that would be sealed up for posterity. They explained that, "A number of lead boxes of different shapes and sizes had been prepared to fit into available spaces enclosed by the steps, and into these were placed various articles contributed by the departments in Washington and by individuals. Applications for space in them came in from all over the country. Some were evidently prompted by vanity, others by a hope of advertisement, but the majority was based on a commonsense desire to perpetuate some examples of our civilization."

When all was said and done and "Cleopatra's Needle" arrived, experts were brought in to interpret the hieroglyphics on the four sides. *The Evening Post* interpreted them, in contemporary themes, in an article on November 3, 1880, even before the obelisk was erected.

Four months later (or one hundred twelve days to be precise), after the initial rolling of the obelisk, the incredible journey was nearly at an end. It arrived at its permanent site, immediately behind the Metropolitan Museum of Art, and had to be transferred to the pedestal that would be its final resting place.

The granite base, on which the monument would rest, was said to be "the largest and heaviest stone ever moved [except for the obelisk itself] on wheels." It required thirty-two horses in sixteen pairs to put it in place. Blocks and stairs were engineered beforehand. According to plan, "The foundation was replaced exactly as it had stood in Alexandria, Egypt, 3,500 years before, each piece in the same relative position to the others."

On February 22, 1881, in the Grand Hall of the Metropolitan Museum of Art, the gift of "Cleopatra's Needle" was formally presented to the City of New York. During the four months that it took to move the obelisk across Manhattan Island, the anticipation of its arrival at its final resting place had been building. As the crowd surged to get a closer look, the *New York Herald* stated that the excitement was like "a favorite opera night, ten times intensified." The president of the Metropolitan Museum of Art, John Tyler Johnson, made the opening remarks. The effort to bring "the Needle" across the island of Manhattan was no small task, and Johnson commended the efforts of all those involved. The assembled dignitaries, guests, and curious onlookers cheered their approval.

But there was one final obstacle to overcome. How would this 3,500-year-old, 224-ton piece of antiquity be set into its permanent position? The engineers involved had planned for this moment for months. They knew that they would have only one chance to do it right. If they failed, the obelisk could fall, smashing it beyond repair. All the ropes and pulleys were checked to make sure that there was just the right balance between tension and slack. Henry Gorringe checked his final calculations and then gave the order: "Hoist it, gentlemen." All it took was fifteen minutes for "Cleopatra's Needle" to be set firmly on its base. Again, the crowd roared its approval. They had done it! They had successfully transported a piece of antiquity all the way from Alexandria, Egypt, to New York City and had set it up for all to admire.

Many years later, the famous film producer Cecil B. DeMille, best known for his epic movie *The Ten Commandments,* spent his own money to have the hieroglyphics interpreted. The hieroglyphics cover four panels of the obelisk and each set refers to something different in regards to worship of the Egyptian gods. Being a native New Yorker, DeMille spent many happy days in this area of Central Park and wanted to give back to the community.

Today, "Cleopatra's Needle" still stands proudly behind the Metropolitan Museum of Art, just the way it was erected in 1881, but it is often missed by visitors. So the next time you are in Central Park on a bright sunny day and you see a giant shadow, take the time to walk up the stairs and get a look at "Cleopatra's Needle" firsthand. Remember all the effort and ingenuity that it took to bring it here so that New Yorkers could have their piece of history.

TEN DAYS IN AN ASYLUM

1887

Nellie Bly stood before her mirror making deranged faces. She turned up the gas in her room to make her eyes bulge. She read ghost stories to put her in a fearful state. She practiced until she felt she perfected it. She then checked herself into the Temporary Home for Females, a boarding house at 84 Second Avenue. She told them she was looking for work. But in truth, she planned to go insane.

She was accepted into a double room for thirty cents a night. She put her stuff in her room, took a deep breath, and was ready. She headed downstairs donned in old clothes. As she sat to eat dinner with the rest of the boarders, she would glance at them suspiciously. She told the head matron that she was afraid of them. She broke into sobs at one point.

When it was time to go to bed, she refused. She told the head matron that she thought everyone there was crazy and she was scared to sleep. The other boarders tried to calm Nellie down, but the more they did, the more paranoid Nellie would act. Her roommate witnessed Nellie sitting at the edge of the bed the entire night just staring. The women in the place were frightened, and one had a nightmare that she would murder them all.

The next morning the assistant matron called the police. They escorted Nellie to the Essex Market Police courtroom. A kindly looking Judge Duffy asked her name. "Nellie Brown," she replied.

"Where do you come from?"

"Cuba," she said.

"Why did you come to New York?"

"I didn't come to New York, I'm looking for my trunks." He then asked a series of questions to which she feigned amnesia, stared aimlessly, and would repeat, "I can't remember. I can't remember." The judge concluded that this "mysterious waif" had been drugged and brought to the city.

He ordered Nellie be examined by several doctors at Bellevue, the holding pen for the insane asylum. He instructed them to be kind to her as she looked like a good girl. Upon their expert opinion he would decide what to do with her.

For several days doctors would ask Nellie (and every other patient in the holding pen) the same questions. "Do you see faces on the walls? Do you hear voices? What do they say?" Each patient denied it. But those were the only questions asked. One doctor made Nellie stretch her arms out and wiggle her fingers. She did and he responded, "Hopeless!" The head of the insane pavilion of Bellevue hospital gave his verdict: "She is undoubtedly insane."

With that, police escorted Nellie via ambulance to a boat that took her into the Women's Lunatic Asylum on Blackwell Island, a 120-acre of land in the East River, which housed 1,600 supposedly insane women.

Her incarceration caught the attention of the media. The *New York Sun* wrote, "Who is this Insane Girl?"

Meanwhile the editor and owner, Joseph Pulitzer of the famed *New York World* newspaper, was smiling like a Cheshire cat. You see, the mysterious waif, Elizabeth Jane Cochrane, had appeared in his office on September 22, 1887. Elizabeth, whose pen name (as was the custom of women writers of the time) was Nellie Bly, was a journalist, author, daredevil, and feminist. She had just come off a stint where she spent six months in Mexico, where she uncovered and wrote about the plight of working women and Mexico's dictatorship. She was threatened with arrest so she quickly left and headed back to the States, where she got a job with the *Pittsburgh Dispatch* reporting on arts and theater. But she got bored. So she went to New York and applied for the job at the *New York World*. Pulitzer told her she could have the job if she agreed to go undercover and feign insanity to investigate the reports of brutality and neglect that were coming out of the asylum. Within a day Nellie started her undercover work. She had some doubts at first. "Could I assume the characteristics of insanity to such a degree that I could pass the doctors, live for a week among the insane without the authorities there finding out? . . . I said I believed I could."

She had to carefully and without notice chronicle the inside workings. Her last question to the editor was, "How will you get me out?" He said, "I do not know, but we will get you out if we have to tell who you are and for what purpose you feigned insanity—only get in."

"From the moment I entered the insane ward on the Island, I made no attempt to keep up the assumed role of insanity. I talked and acted just as I do in ordinary life. Yet strange to say, the more sanely I talked and acted, the crazier I was thought to be by all except one physician, whose kindness and gentle ways I shall not soon forget."

For ten days Nellie witnessed it all: the fifty-two "really insane woman" who were kept on an ironclad rope; the cold, bug-infested meals that they were forced to eat without knives and forks (those without teeth went without eating); the daily routine where the patients were forced to sit erect in straight-back benches from 6:00 a.m. till 8:00 p.m. and were not allowed to talk, read, move, get up, stretch, or sit sideways. Nellie wrote, "What, excepting torture, would produce insanity quicker than this treatment?"

The living conditions were just as bad. The place was bitter cold. The nurses were bundled up in coats, and the sixty women in that wing were all bathed in one ice-cold bathtub, with buckets poured on their heads. The filthy tub water wasn't changed till it was thick black. There were two combs for sixty women. Anyone who complained of the cold was beaten. Nellie witnessed the nurses teasing a seventy-year-old blind woman by putting their hands inside her thin garment. She watched a nurse drag an old gray-haired woman into a closet, where she heard the pleadings, the screams, and eventually silence. Another woman was punched and given a black eye. Patients begged for water for a whole night and not one drop was given to them.

Each day was identical. Many prayed for death. When Nellie complained to the doctors, they just took notes and nodded. If the patients were really "troublesome," they were sent to the "Retreat." Nellie befriended many women who she believed were just as sane as she was. She jotted down Retreat accounts. One Mrs. Cotter described her story: "For crying the nurses beat me with a broom handle and jumped on me, injuring me internally, so that I shall never get over it. Then they tied my hands and feet and, throwing a sheet over my head, twisted it tightly around my throat, so I could not scream, and thus put me in a bathtub filled with cold water. They held me under until I gave up every hope and became senseless. At other times they took hold of my ears and beat my head on the floor and against the wall. Then they pulled out my hair by the roots, so that it will never grow in again."

As the patients all said, "It was hopeless to complain to the doctors, for they always said it was the imagination of our diseased brains."

In another instance, a young sick girl was beaten, then put naked in a cold bath, then thrown on her bed. "When morning came, the girl was dead. The doctors said she died of convulsions, and that was all that was done about it."

Nellie herself was not beaten because the press was still watching, trying to figure out who this insane girl from Cuba was. On the tenth day, as promised, the editor got her out. "A lawyer, Peter A. Hendricks, came and told me that friends of mine were willing to take charge of me if I would rather be with them than in the asylum. I was only too glad to give my consent. Sadly I said farewell to all I knew as I passed them on my way to freedom and life, while they were left behind to a fate worse than death."

Soon after her release Nellie was summoned to testify in front of a grand jury. The district attorney and jurors wanted Nellie to accompany them on a trip to the asylum. No one was supposed to know of the trip, but word leaked. All the women who had been beaten had mysteriously disappeared; the place had been cleaned up. Nellie worried for the well-being of those women and wondered if the jury would believe her.

However, conflicting testimonies from the nurses made the jurors suspicious.

The jurors believed Nellie Bly and reported to the court that things must be changed. One million dollars was given for the benefit of the insane.

After her undercover work, she wrote a series of articles for *The World*. The first was titled "Behind Asylum Bars" and ran on October 9, 1887. Nellie Bly was permitted to sign her name to the story. The signing was a Pulitzer innovation. Up until then most columnists were not allowed to sign their names, much less a woman and a newcomer. This catapulted her into fame. She went on to write a book titled *Ten Days in the Madhouse,* which was sold for twenty-five cents, complete with illustrations.

POLAR BEAR CLUBS

1903 and 2009

There was an air of excitement as about fifty adults stripped down to their tiny bathing suits. The temperature was about thirty degrees, and the water temperature was about the same. The sun was shining on the snow-covered sandy beach. Is this now or is this 1903? The place: historic Coney Island, named after a type of rabbit that was common in that area. But no one was looking at rabbits that day. Coney Island, famous home to the landmark Cyclone Roller Coaster, the parachute ride, and the original Nathan's hot dogs, had something much more bizarre going on.

As the group walked frigidly down the beach, they formed a long triple row of bodies in all shapes and sizes. Most of them were shirtless, and a few appeared to have on sweaters. However, if you looked closer, these "sweaters" were actually body hair! These hardy souls encompassed a wide range of vocations: everything from lawyers, corporate vice presidents, teachers, fast talkers, computer company owners (one whose brother happened to be an astronaut and actually participated in this event himself), and a variety of others too numerous to elaborate on. The one common bond they had was the pure enthusiasm they all possessed. They all wanted to jump into this freezing water in the dead of winter! You couldn't help but smile as you witnessed their collective zeal!

Whenever reporters interviewed these people, the first question always was, "Why would anyone subject themselves to this type of torture? Why do this?" Health was the universal response. Contrary to what many of us have been told by our mothers, many of the participants said that they hadn't been sick since they started engaging in this invigorating activity, and for some of them, this was twenty years or more. One individual, computer company owner Frank LaFauci, had traveled from Stamford, Connecticut, to attempt his first plunge. He said, "I always wanted to know what it felt like if I was ever in an accident and stranded in the water" (like Leonardo DiCaprio at the end of *Titanic*). Just watching Frank, clothed in his bathing suit and diving slippers, plunging into the thirty-degree water of the Atlantic Ocean, made you shiver!

To understand the mentality of the Polar Bear Club members, you must go back in time to New Year's Day in 1903 and look at the man who started it all. The Polar Bear Club was founded by book, magazine, and newspaper entrepreneur and self-made millionaire Bernarr (because someone misspelled his given name, Bernard, and he liked it so much he decided to change it permanently) MacFadden. MacFadden was the original "Mr. Physical Culture," sort of like a Jack LaLanne and Charles Atlas (Angelo Siciliano) rolled into one hyped and sensationalistic package. At five feet six inches and one hundred forty pounds, he loved posing nude for all who were willing to gawk. Bernarr MacFadden was the owner of the Roaring Twenties' most decadent tabloid, *True Story Magazine*. He was a man with little formal education, born in the Ozark Mountains, who believed that he could be the President of the United States, if he so desired.

In his publication *Physical Culture,* MacFadden would often show how his healthy lifestyle and daily ritual of fasting and taking cold-water plunges would rid him of harmful germs and illnesses. On New Year's Day 1903, Bernarr decided to take fifty believers in his cold-water philosophy and take the plunge. When MacFadden entered the icy Atlantic water on that winter day in 1903, he was demonstrating one of his most important principles: that plunges into cold water can jump-start the body, improve circulation, and improve overall health. He knew that he would have his share of critics, and he would have to answer a lot of questions regarding this practice.

That day he created not only a yearly ritual that continues to this day, adopted by dozens of chapters of Polar Bear Clubs all over the world, but also a Physical Culture Creed, which stated: "We believe that our bodies are the most glorious possessions; that health-wealth is our greatest asset; that every influence which interferes with the attainment of superb, buoyant health should be recognized as a menace. We maintain that weakness is truly a crime; that sickness is the penalty of violated health laws; that every man can be a vigorous vital specimen of masculinity; that every woman can be a splendidly strong, well-poised specimen of femininity. . ."

Not much has changed in over a hundred of years. Members of the present-day Coney Island Polar Bear Club are often looked at by outsiders as nuts. One of the most common questions is, "Can't you get hypothermia?" The Polar Bears admit that it could happen, but since there is so much camaraderie and everyone looks out for each other, this has not been a problem.

So what is the proper Polar Bear plunge attire? Other than bathing suits (MacFadden may have done this in the nude, but the witnesses didn't tell), surf or diving boots are recommended, more to protect your feet from sharp objects on the ocean bottom than from the cold water (nothing really keeps the cold from affecting you!). And of course, one of the most important questions of all, especially among male plungers, is, "What about shrinkage!?" The members like to use this old chant to answer the question: "Shrinkage comes and shrinkage goes, Monday morning no one knows!" They challenge everyone to personally come to Coney Island and find out.

The day's events before the hardy souls enter the water are quite simple. They usually do a lot of warm-up exercises, accompanied by hand clapping, singing, shouting, and anything that will get them fired up (no pun intended) to enter the icy water. Most of the participants go in willingly, but others need a little coaxing or escorting. Individuals who have taken the plunge have had a variety of reactions to the experience. One person, who was obviously not very happy, said, "I'm frozen. It's like walking on cement." Another person, an initial skeptic, commented after the experience, "Honestly, it feels refreshing. It's not that bad." Another similar comment was, "In a weird way, it feels really great even though it's really painful. It's a weird balance!" Our fellow coauthor, Fran Capo, has done it twice (once in New York and once in Antarctica) and said, "It's like getting a really bad ice cream headache . . . it comes on quickly, goes away in a minute, and then you really enjoy the results."

The die-hards, like Coney Island Polar member Louie Scarcella, have only the most positive things to say. "We believe that swimming in the cold water once a week or more strengthens the immune system, makes you strong. It takes away all the pain in your body."

From 1903 to 2009, many changes have taken place in New York City, but many things have remained the same. The city has always been home to a variety of people with a variety of interests. It is the place where most new things are tried first and a place where traditions are held in high regard. The beach is still the beach, and the waters of the Atlantic still are icy in the winter. Coney Island is the place where Bernarr MacFadden first ran into that icy water, and it is still the place where people who have the same zest for life and enjoy that exhilarating thrill take the plunge on those cold winter days.

THE TRIAL OF THE CENTURY, OR THREE'S A CROWD

1906

It was the hot summer night of June 25, 1906. Evelyn (Nesbit) Thaw was getting ready for a night out with her husband, Harry Thaw. While she bathed, her husband left their room in the Hotel Lorraine and walked four blocks to the corner of Forty-forth and Fifth to a bar called Sherry's. He was wearing a straw hat and a long black overcoat. The hatcheck girl offered to take his coat, but he was adamant about keeping it. He then downed three whiskies, paid for it with a one hundred dollar bill, and walked back to the hotel. He instructed his chauffeur to follow him in his touring car. He picked up his wife from the hotel, and from there they went to the Café Martins on Twenty-sixth Street between Broadway and Fifth to meet another couple they were dining with. They were ushered to their table, and Thaw sat with his back to the room. His wife sat opposite him where she could see the parade of who's who coming to dine. At one point, she glanced up and saw her former lover, famed architect Stanford White. She paused very subtly and then continued talking.

Jealous Thaw noticed this and asked what was the matter. She tried to pass it off. Thaw persisted, making their guests uncomfortable. Mrs. Thaw passed him a note under the table that said, "That B is here." Thaw immediately started biting his fingernails and fidgeting. He got a glazed look in his eyes. Conversation stopped. Fearful that Thaw would fly into one of his public rages, she excused themselves from dinner under the guise of being late for the play they were going to see that night at Madison Square Garden.

With the chauffeur following them, they briskly walked the four blocks to the Garden, one of White's structures. They took the elevator to the rooftop, where hundreds were in attendance to watch the open-air premiere of the musical *Mamzelle Champagne*.

The musical had started. White's usual table by the stage was still empty. At 10:55 p.m., during the song "I Could Love a Thousand Girls," Thaw spotted White making his way to his table. White greeted people as he passed.

Ten minutes later during a dueling scene on stage, Thaw was within feet of White's table. White felt his presence and turned to face him. Thaw pulled out a gun. White half rose, and in cold blood, Thaw shot White three times in the face, only inches from his head. The fatal bullet entered his left eye. White fell back, taking the tablecloth with him. White's face, "blackened with powder burns, slumped forward." At first people thought it was part of the play. But then a woman screamed, the music stopped, glasses crashed to the floor. There was a moment of complete silence and realization. Harry lifted his gun to the ceiling to empty the chambers as he stood over his victim, but by then, everyone was running for the door. The murder was done at 11:05 p.m.

The stage manager ordered the girls to "Dance! Sing! Keep it up!" He yelled to the audience, "It's all right. It's all right. Ladies and gentlemen, a serious accident has occurred. Please leave the house as quietly as possible." Women fainted. One man pronounced White dead; a waiter pulled a tablecloth over White's face, but blood soaked through it and he had to place another one on top of the first.

Thaw was still standing over the body with the smoking gun in his hand. Paul Brudi, a fireman on duty at the Garden, walked over to Thaw and took the revolver from him. Staring blankly at the fireman, Thaw said, "He ruined my wife. He deserved it and I can prove it." Brudi walked Thaw to the elevator, at which point Officer Anthony L. Debes announced, "You're under arrest."

Mrs. Thaw made her way to the elevator as the doors closed.

She turned to her handcuffed husband and asked, "Why did you do it that way?" Thaw smiled, "Don't worry, everything will be all right." Upon his request, she then kissed him. He was counting on his incredible wealth to buy the best attorneys, psychologists, and witnesses. The next few weeks proved him right.

It was known as the crime of the century, a "trial reported to the ends of the civilized globe," according to the *New York Times*. It was a crime that had every ingredient sure to sell thousands of newspapers; passion, wealth, jealousy, beauty, and deceit spun from a hatred from two men competing for the affections of a poor child turned "America's prettiest girl model" and showgirl, Evelyn Nesbit.

In one corner, fifty-two-year-old, red-haired Stanford White, New York's top architect, who had built the second Madison Square Garden, the New York Herald Building, Penn Station, the Arch in Washington Square Park, the Century Club, and the uptown campus of NYU, along with a thousand other works over a twenty-five-year career with his firm. He was well liked, eccentric, the desired guest of every "in" party of the new rich, inventor of the banquet, generous, never lost his temper, and moved at a fast pace. He was a creative genius who had taken Nesbit under his wing as a mistress, helped build her career, educated her, dressed her in the finest clothes, paid for an apartment for her and her mother, and eventually, when she had fallen in love with him, "stole" her virginity at the age of sixteen.

In the other corner sat Harry Thaw, millionaire playboy heir to the vast Pittsburgh railway fortune, suspicious, jealous, and nicknamed "Mad Harry" by the other showgirls. He was someone who didn't like being snubbed or taking no for an answer. He had displayed some "odd" behavior in public like lighting cigars with hundred-dollar bills, holding parties for four hundred chorus girls, bestowing on them each a plateful of diamonds. He was blacklisted from White's parties because of his behavior. He hated White's success and wanted what he had. He hired a detective to follow White's every move, and even reported White to the Suppression of Vice Commission, stating White had "drugged and ravaged 378 virgins." Feeling inferior, he was obsessed with destroying White.

While Nesbit was White's longtime mistress, Thaw took a liking to her. Sneakily Thaw courted her under an alias, "Mr. Monroe." Nesbit avoided him, commenting, "He scares me to death." But his persistence, her plan to try to make White jealous, and several persuasive ambassadors and heiresses to plead his case eventually convinced Nesbit at the age of nineteen to leave White and marry Thaw, despite Thaw having brutally beaten her on several occasions with a whip after admitting she lost her virginity to White. Nesbit's mother bitterly disapproved of the marriage. Nesbit wore black to her own wedding. From that moment on, Thaw insisted that Nesbit refer to White as the "Beast" (B) and to always let him know if she saw him. That night she did.

Nesbit's love for White, and anger at herself for not being able to "capture him," made her do things to enrage Thaw. She would often tell Thaw, "White treated me better than you do. He gave me better presents. He is different." She played on Thaw's jealousy, which led to continued bouts of cocaine use, beatings, and then groveling public apologies. Harry was obsessed with Nesbit staying with him.

While Thaw was imprisoned at the Tombs on Murders Row, Mother Thaw put up a million dollars to save her son from the electric chair and an equal amount to "dissuade witnesses." The law firm of Black, Olcott, Gruber, and Bonynge was hired. A press agent was hired to feed the newspapers the story of the "honorable husband defending his wife's honor."

Meanwhile, from his cell, Thaw was enjoying the attention, telling reporters how White ravaged young girls. Reporters went to get quotes from White's friends, who all went underground at the request of Mrs. White, plus none of the rich wanted their secret parties and reputations scrutinized, leaving newspapers with only one side of the story to tell, Thaw's, making him a hero.

Luckily some of the chorus girls came forward and said that anyone who was with White at his parties did it willingly and were treated kindly and respectfully.

Mother Thaw's money squashed many of the reports of the behaviors of her abuser son, like the time he beat a bellboy in his tub and then rubbed salt in the wound because he delivered the wrong food, or the chorus girls he tied up and beat with a whip. His servant disposed of his drug paraphernalia and bag of whips. Mother Thaw agreed to pay Nesbit a sum of $1 million for her testimony, knowing a well-rehearsed story would be the key to getting Thaw off death row. Nesbit agreed. The payment issue of course came out after the trial.

The case of *People v. Harry k. Thaw* opened on January 23, 1907. Over ten thousand people waited outside to catch a glimpse of Nesbit. Inside over one hundred reporters were in attendance. An unprecedented eight days of jury selection began, with Nesbit giving the yea or nay on instinct who would believe her. Note: Many factors come into play when choosing a jury . . . for example, Dr. Phil of TV fame, prior to TV, was hired to analyze the psychological makeup of individual jurors, thus allowing him to select which jurors would be good for a certain side of the case.

William T. Jerome was the prosecuting district attorney. He was a well-respected, just judge turned district attorney. He was a common man, and the term "Go to Jerome" meant you would get a fair trial. On the other side were the five high-priced defense lawyers. Leading the team was Mr. Delphin Michael Delmas, who had worked for weeks on Nesbit's testimony, down to the suit and hat she was to wear to court.

Nesbit wore an outfit that made her look like a virginal schoolgirl (despite her secret three abortions) and a black velvet hat trimmed with violets. Before the jury selection was done, this hat became the new fashion on the streets of New York.

Each side had its problems: DA Jerome would have gladly accepted an insanity plea, but once the jury was selected and a plea of "not guilty" was entered, he had to prove beyond a shadow of a doubt that the murder of White was premeditated and in the first degree.

Delmas, the defense attorney, also wanted to enter an insanity plea, but Thaw insisted he was sane. So Delmas had to say he was only temporarily insane when he shot White; the medical term "brainstorm" was coined to describe his insanity. Anyone who knew Thaw knew that he was a bona fide nut case all year-round.

The day Nesbit took the stand you could hear a pin drop, and despite Jerome's objections that Nesbit's story was hearsay, the judge allowed it, saying she was only telling the court what she had told Thaw that led to his "brainstorm," aka temporary insanity.

Nesbit testified about the night White "attacked" her as Thaw cried at the defense table. As instructed by Delmas, she carefully left out that she was in love with White, that it was consensual, and that Stanford White charmed her.

Then other defense witness testified that, "Come up to see my etchings" was a line that Stanford White coined to woo girls. The once heroic DA Jerome was so angered at Nesbit's lies, he lost his composure in court, got reprimanded by the judge, and forgot to ask witnesses pertinent questions.

At one point, Nesbit's own mother was willing to testify on White's behalf, showing letters that he was a good man whom her daughter loved, but $50,000 of Thaw's money got that urge to disappear. There was even an affidavit that Nesbit had signed in White's attorney's office stating that Thaw had brutally beaten her; that, however, was not admitted into court.

The jury had to decide. Frustrated, Jerome's closing argument was this: "Will you acquit a cold-blooded, deliberate, cowardly murderer because his lying wife has a pretty girl's face?"

The jury was sequestered for seventy-three days. They came back with a hung jury.

Thaw spent 1907 in jail while a second trial was formed.

This time, with a new defense attorney, they changed the grounds to permanent insanity. At the second trial Thaw was found not guilty and committed to the Asylum for the Criminally Insane at Matteawan.

Although Thaw boasted as he left the courtroom that he was indeed sane and his attorneys would have him out in a "matter of weeks," he spent seven years in the asylum. He was treated royally while there: He was permitted to leave the asylum, received free food compliments of Delmonico's, and the crowds loved him.

As for Nesbit, the Thaw family never paid her what they promised. Right after her testimony in the second trial, she filed for divorce. She had no money, became a vaudeville dancer, opened several speakeasies, had a son from Thaw that she claimed she conceived during one of her conjugal visits, and got remarried. On her deathbed she admitted that Stanford White was the only man she ever loved.

TERRORIST ATTACK ON
WALL STREET

1920

It was business as usual in downtown Manhattan on September 16, 1920. There in the area simply known as "The Corner" located on Wall and Broad Street stood three impressive buildings: To the south on 23 Wall Street stood a fortresslike structure, the world's most powerful financial institution, the banking firm of J. P. Morgan and Company, aka "The House of Morgan." To the north stood the U.S. Assay Office, where $900 million in gold bars were being moved by workers that day, and next to it was the U.S. Sub-treasury building (today called Federal Hall) with an impressive statue of George Washington in front. A block away was the New York Stock Exchange. It was the busiest corner of America's financial center, and it was just coming of age.

It was lunchtime. A beautiful clear day where everyone wanted to get out and about. The Trinity Church bells were chiming. A pair of young sisters, Margaret and Charity Bishop, met for lunch, excited to talk about their new job that was helping them support their widowed mother. A peddler by the name of Lawrence Servin was selling chocolates while keeping an eye out for the cops. Dozens of horse carts were on the street, enticing workers to buy their wares. Others were headed to the stock exchange carrying pouches of valuable securities. The street was filled with messengers, stenographers, clerks, secretaries, bank tellers, and brokers, the average middle-class Americans trying to make a living. Some were American born; others were from Sweden, Poland, England, and Ireland.

At noon, Lawrence Servin noticed a "dark-complexioned, unshaven, wiry man, probably around thirty-five or forty years old, dressed in working clothes and a dark cap" pull up in a dilapidated horse-drawn wooden buggy. He eyed the man to see if he was competition. But the driver quickly got out and scurried away. It was now 12:01 and the church bells stopped ringing.

For a moment there was silence and then BOOM! Lawrence was flung into the air and knocked unconscious. A hundred pounds of dynamite packed with five hundred pounds of small cast-iron slugs called sash weights, which had been wired to a timer that was sitting in the back of that horse-drawn wagon, exploded. All that remained in its place were the jawbone of the horse and two charred horse hooves still wearing their shoes.

But the damage went far beyond that. In seconds, "a mushroom-shaped cloud of yellowish green smoke" shot up 100 feet. Awnings as high as up to the twelfth floor caught fire and disintegrated. The explosion tossed an automobile twenty feet into the air and overturned many others. Windows shattered in a half-mile radius, turning broken glass into missiles mutilating bodies on the busy streets below. The iron slugs acted as shrapnel, leaving the streets red with human and animal blood. Body parts were flung everywhere; scalps were torn off heads, a single horse leg landed on the steps of one building, a women's head still wearing a hat was lodged into a wall, on the steps of the Morgan bank lay a mutilated body of a man. One body, half-naked with burns, started to rise up only to fall lifeless face down in the gutter. Many bodies lay dead as a stampede of people ran for their lives. Thirty-eight people were killed instantly, and four hundred more were injured, one of them being Junuis Morgan, Jack Morgan's son. Jack himself was in Europe on a business trip. The only person killed inside the firm was a twenty-four-year-old clerk, William Joyce, who was supposed to have been on his honeymoon but had postponed his wedding to cover for a coworker who was on vacation. Only seven of the dead were over the age of forty. Two million dollars worth of property was destroyed.

Within minutes, a bell rang out on the New York Stock Exchange floor, halting trade for the first time ever due to violence. Seventeen hundred New York City cops and firemen and seventy-five Red Cross nurses raced to the scene by horse, car, subway, and foot. Soon after troops from the 22nd Infantry, which were stationed on Governor's Island, marched through lower Manhattan with their rifles and bayonets ready to take on another attack and restore some order. The mayor, John Hylan, rushed to the site to supervise. People started helping. A seventeen-year-old boy, James Saul, commandeered a car, loaded it with injured people, and drove them to Broad Street Hospital.

Refusing to be deterred by the terrorist act, the NYSE governors met at 3:30 p.m. and decided to open the area the next day for business. A cleanup was quickly started; bodies were laid out on the sidewalk covered with car blankets, torn awnings, or whatever could be found. In an effort to "get things back to normal," valuable physical evidence that could have led to the culprits was tossed into garbage bins. Detectives had to stop trucks to retrieve evidence.

By nightfall the head of the Justice Department Bureau of Investigation, William Flynn, along with several federal detectives, had arrived in New York.

One warning letter was found in a mailbox a block away from the explosion. Since the mailbox was emptied around 11:30 each day, detectives figured the message was dropped on the way to detonating the bomb. The warning was stamped on an ordinary piece of paper with a rubber printing kit.

The letter read, "Remember. We will not tolerate any longer. Free the political prisoners or it will be death for all of you. American Anarchist Fighters!" (The previous day, the infamous anarchists Sacco and Vanzetti had been indicted for bank robbery and murder.)

The note was analyzed, and even though its language structure was similar to other "bomb" leaflets, it was deemed insufficient evidence. The *Washington Post* declared this bombing an "act of war."

Italian anarchists, especially the Galleanists (followers of Luigi Galleani), were their top suspect. One member in particular, Mario Buda, an associate of Sacco and Vanzetti who was experienced in the use of dynamite and explosives used in construction and who was also in the city at the time, seemed a likely suspect but returned to Italy after the bombing, and was beyond the reach of the Bureau of Investigation. He was never arrested or even questioned by police. It was believed that Galleani himself ordered the strike, but he too was on Italian soil.

The next day, however, despite the investigation and devastation, Wall Street was up and functioning. Everyone was back at their desks, complete with bruises and bandages. The only difference was heightened security. New Yorkers were defiant and patriotic and as the *Sun* and *New York Herald* put it, people were "determined to show the world that business would proceed as usual despite bombs." Surprisingly, volume on the stock exchange was high; some stocks even rose in value.

At noon, thousands gathered and, led by the Sons of the American Revolution, sang "America the Beautiful," and a previously planned celebration took place in front of the George Washington statue as scheduled.

Meanwhile the police were tracking down every lead they could find. Witnesses were spoken to; the charred horse hooves and shoes were brought around to hundreds of stables to discover who purchased the horse and buggy, but nothing was determined. They hauled in well-known anarchists and even questioned Edward Fischer, a former NYC tennis champion who apparently predicted the bombings in postcards. However, he was deemed mentally unbalanced and sent to Bellevue.

Within days of the attack, a mobilization occurred. Congress and the Department of Justice were called upon to increase funding and enact drastic laws to counter the threat of the Communists and Anarchists. Renewed investigation into the movements of foreign radicals was opened, creating the development of the U.S. Justice Department's General Intelligence Division of the Bureau of Investigation (the forerunner of the FBI).

Initially citizens were patriotic and vowed revenge against the attackers. But soon critics claimed the government was using the terrorist threats as a way to cut down on civil liberties. Some wrote that an aggressive action against the terrorists would cause more violence and ruin America's reputation in Europe. Others claimed the President was just a puppet and government officials twisted the reports to carry out their own agenda.

The case was investigated for over three years, but it produced nothing . . . no indictments, no trials, no culprits. No one took responsibility for the crime, and nothing was left to indicate what or who its intended target was.

Nine years after the attack, Sidney Sutherland wrote in *Liberty* magazine, "If the Wall Street bomb explosion was the result of a murder plot, it speaks eloquently for the bond of silence which the lawless world imposes on its members."

Decades later the FBI said that they believed their initial thoughts were correct and that a small group of Italian Anarchists were to blame, but there was no evidence to prove it. The FBI made the file inactive in 1940, and the case is still considered officially unsolved. The only thing that remains as a reminder is the visible scars. If you walk past 23 Wall Street and check out the lower facade of the building, it still bears the moonlike craters and pockmarks of what marked the Ground Zero of that era, only blocks away from the Ground Zero of today.

THE DEATH OF THE SHEIK

1926

On Monday August 23, 1926, at 12:10 p.m., a strikingly handsome young man, age thirty-one, died in New York's Polyclinic Hospital. He had been given the last rites at 10:00 a.m., when his death seemed imminent. Nurses wept quietly, waiting for the inevitable to happen. Normally this would not have been news, but this was no ordinary young man. His name was Rodolpho Alfonzo Rafaelo Pierre Filibert Guglielmi di Valentina d'Antonguollo—better known to the world as Rudolph Valentino.

A few weeks earlier, Valentino had begun a cross-country tour to promote his latest movie, *The Son of the Sheik*. On August 15, 1926, while in New York City, he was suddenly taken ill and rushed to Polyclinic Hospital, complaining of severe abdominal pain. He was immediately sent for X-rays, and the results confirmed a perforated ulcer. Surgery was performed to clean out the abdominal cavity and repair the ulcer. At first, it seemed as if the surgery was a success and Valentino would make a complete recovery. But this was not to be! Within several days his gut became swollen and his skin around the point of the incision began to look bruised and blotchy. Additional X-rays were ordered and the worst fears of the doctors were realized—an infection had set in. The doctors procrastinated for several hours, debating over what to do next, which only worsened their patient's condition. Whether it was botched surgery, poor after-surgery care, or, as some speculate, reluctance to be "the *one* who cut open Valentino," nothing further was done. Within hours, "The Great Lover" was dead.

Hordes of people had gathered outside Polyclinic Hospital waiting for word as to what had happened to the actor. As soon as the news of his death came to light, the rumors began. Some felt that Valentino was poisoned or perhaps shot by a jealous husband or one of his many former lovers. Almost immediately, pandemonium broke loose. Within a few hours, two young women outside the hospital attempted suicide, and a young boy in another part of the city died on a bed covered with Valentino photos. As far away as London, another woman took poison in front of a picture of the late, great "Sheik."

A short time later, Valentino's body was placed in a plain wicker basket, covered with a gold cloth. It was removed from the hospital and taken to the premier funeral home in New York City, Frank E. Campbell's (other notable funerals at Campbell's include Judy Garland, Jacqueline Kennedy Onassis, John Lennon, Luther Vandross, and Heath Ledger) on Sixty-sixth Street and Broadway. At about 2:00 p.m. the morticians began their work. Valentino's body had to be embalmed and then prepared for his last appearance before his adoring public. The process took many hours, and according to Campbell's spokesmen, the body was not treated any differently than any other (which seems a bit hard to believe). As Valentino's body was being prepared for viewing, the crowd outside the funeral home began to grow. It took on a carnival-like atmosphere. There were reports (though unsubstantiated) that the morticians feared the body of Valentino might be defaced in some way during the viewing, so they decided to take a drastic precaution. According to a source, they would not display the real Rudolph Valentino. "To save the idol from wear and tear, Valentino was substituted by a wax dummy for the body—an artist was called in who was skilled at creating a perfect likeness. So while the real Valentino lay in peace in a cool, dark vault, the wax figure of Valentino took the brutal punishment from the hundreds of fans at the funeral parlor."

No one was able to tell if it was the real Valentino or a wax image (except maybe an expert from Madame Tussaud's). The Valentino that greeted his onlookers was dressed in a dinner jacket, had heavy pancake makeup and mascara applied to his face, and had a seductive smile curling his lips. Gone was all the warmth and passion that he exuded in life. The charismatic fire that made him a star and great screen idol was now just a memory. He was in a bronze, glass-enclosed casket on a raised pedestal. There was also a low railing and a cushioned ledge where people could kneel and pray. Thousands of flowers surrounded the casket, including four thousand red roses sent by actress Pola Negri, from Hollywood. Negri claimed that she was secretly engaged to Valentino, and the couple planned to make the announcement after his return from the publicity tour for *The Son of the Sheik*. (No one knows if her claim was true; however, she did put on a good show when Valentino was later put in a crypt at his final resting place in the Hollywood Forever Cemetery, by "fainting" several times!)

By the time things were in place for the public viewing, the crowd outside had grown to thirty thousand and was becoming quite anxious and unruly. No one at the Frank E. Campbell Funeral Home or anyone from the New York City Police Department anticipated the chaotic scene about to unfold. The crowd began to push and shove in hopes of getting a better place in line for the viewing. Several people were thrown to the ground, and many others were stepped on or kicked in the process. Clothing was torn and personal items such as hats, purses, and shoes were literally pulled off their wearers. The surging crowd grew so large that people were pushed into two large plate glass windows, which shattered under the massive weight. When the mourners actually got inside the funeral home, things did not get much better.

For several hours the police could not gain control of the situation. They claimed that they had never seen such rioting in New York City, either in numbers or in behavior. Finally the police commissioner, George McLaughlin, personally took charge and calmed people down a bit.

Around 11:00 p.m. the police tried to break up the crowd and call it a night. But the crowd did not like that option. To avoid more riots, the funeral home remained open until midnight, at which point people were told to come back the next day.

The undertakers at the funeral home were exhausted. Just as they were about to close down for the night, they received some unexpected visitors. Ten men in black shirts announced that they represented the Fascist League of North America and they had come to guard Valentino's body overnight. They further informed the morticians that they were directed by the Fascist Party in Italy to look after one of their native sons, and that Premier Mussolini himself was sending a wreath that he expected would be place on the funeral bier. Not wanting any trouble, the Campbell personnel agreed to let them stay as "body" guards.

The next day the police were better prepared. They came out in force, two hundred strong. The city's finest kept the huge crowd moving in an orderly fashion.

On the third day however, the crowd grew so large in size again it was the blob overtaking the city. Finally, the directors of Campbell's funeral home and George Ullman, Valentino's manager, decided that the rest of the viewing would be by invitation only, a final red carpet event for the actor, with a few hundred privileged people coming with invitations in hand (although some women did try to sneak in a back door), including a group from Castellaneta, Italy, Valentino's hometown.

By all accounts, one hundred thousand people viewed Rudolph Valentino's remains. The police estimated that on the first day of "mourning," approximately two hundred people were injured, most not seriously except for one woman who was trampled by a police horse and several who were cut badly when the plate glass windows broke.

On Monday August 30, 1926, funeral services were held for Hollywood's greatest matinee idol at St. Malachi's Church on Forty-ninth Street. The honorary pall bearers were a who's who of Hollywood executives, including the heads of Paramount, MGM, and Loew Corporations, as well as great film actor Douglas Fairbanks Sr. and New York's own mayor, Jimmy Walker. The site of Valentino's final resting place was still not clear at that time. They debated if he should be sent back to Italy, where he would be buried as "a favorite son," or if he should be interred in a crypt owned by the family of his ex-wife, Natacha Rambova, in the Bronx's Woodlawn Cemetery, where he would lay alongside such notables as F. W. Woolworth, Alva Smith Vanderbilt Belmont, Duke Ellington, Fiorello LaGuardia, and innumerable others. In the end, however, it was determined that since Rudolph Valentino lived a legendary Hollywood life, it was only fitting that Hollywood is where he should remain in death—a legend to the end.

AND THE WALL CAME
TUMBLING DOWN

1934

Nelson Rockefeller stared in disbelief at the forty-one-foot by seventeen-foot mural. How could Diego Rivera, the famed artist and Mexican Socialist, do this unfathomable act to him? After all, Nelson's own mother, Abby Aldrich Rockefeller, had befriended the artist and had even become a confidant to the artist's sickly wife, Frida Kahlo. Nelson felt betrayed, he tried to resolve the dispute, and now on the night of February 10, 1934, he peeked once more under the cream-colored canvas that had kept the mural concealed. He could not believe that it would have to come to this end: ultimate destruction.

Nelson was only twenty-six but already had tremendous political ambitions. He was the son of John D. Rockefeller Jr. and Abby Aldrich Rockefeller, the matriarch of the family. John Jr. was often referred to as "Mr. Junior" even though he was the wealthiest man in America. Mr. Junior gave his son, Nelson, the responsibility to work with his mother to assemble all the artwork for the family landmark buildings at

Rockefeller Center, and specifically for 30 Rockefeller Center (the fifth tallest building in New York City), where the great masterpiece mural was to be housed. The entire complex would serve as an entertainment venue, an office venue, and notably, the first indoor mall in America, in which over a quarter million people would come every day either as visitors or workers. The finest sculptors, artists, and craftsmen were brought in to create this eighteen-building complex. Among them was Diego Rivera, considered the world's greatest muralist.

Initially, Nelson and Abby Rockefeller were thrilled with Rivera's work. It was titled *Man at the Crossroads* and portrayed everything positive about American industry and technology. Then the artist took creative license and, without permission, added Vladimir Lenin to the mural. When the Rockefellers saw the "added dimension," they were not pleased. Lenin was the antithesis of everything that the Rockefeller family stood for, and he absolutely could not be a part of their lobby. It was up to Nelson to speak to the artist about rethinking what he wanted to paint in his fresco. The dapper young millionaire went to the unfinished lobby of Rockefeller Center's signature building to discuss a solution to the situation.

Rivera was perched on top of the scaffold when Nelson entered. When the artist heard him, he smiled and carefully came down from his precipice. Nelson stood face to face with a hulking, three-hundred-pound, potbellied, disheveled man. He was wearing dirty, ill-fitting clothes, his pants much too high up on his stomach, and a beat-up hat resembling that of a Mexican cowboy who couldn't afford the price of a proper Stetson. Rockefeller calmly explained to Rivera that Lenin could not be a part of a mural representing American industry. He suggested that the artist could replace the face of Lenin with an anonymous face, representing all the workers of the world. When the other Mexican laborers who were acting as Rivera's helpers heard Rockefeller's suggestion, they immediately announced that they would go on strike if any part of the masterpiece was not according to the artist's wishes. Rivera stood fast, saying that this was "his" interpretation of the subject matter, and he would not change anything about his vision. The two strong personalities had reached an impasse.

After several days, Rivera came up with what he believed was a fair compromise. He said he would put Abraham Lincoln beside Lenin in the fresco, but he would not waver on his right, as a creative interpreter of the American Industrial Revolution, to leave the Socialist leader in the mural. Nelson had to make a decision. The clock was ticking and precious time was being wasted before the scheduled gala opening of Rockefeller Center. The answer: Nelson Rockefeller gave Diego Rivera an ultimatum: remove the Lenin portrait from the fresco, or he was fired from the project.

Rivera would not budge on the issue of Lenin's removal. So, with the mural almost near completion in May 1933, Nelson Rockefeller paid Rivera his fee of $21,000, told him to vacate the premises immediately, and ordered that the fresco be covered, so that the press and the public could not see it. Nothing more was to be done for the moment. As great admirers of Rivera's artistic genius, both Nelson and his mother hoped that maybe the muralist would reconsider his decision and do what needed to be done to allow the project to be completed and displayed for the world to see. A short time later, Diego Rivera returned to Mexico City with his wife and fellow artist, Frida Kahlo. However, his removal from the project created a storm of protests from both fellow artists who supported his right of artistic expression and from radical labor organizations with Socialistic leanings.

As 1933 drew to a close, the impasse was no closer to a resolution than it was in May. Nelson Rockefeller's patience had reached its end and was now replaced by anger. As much as he was a lover of art, he was left no choice in this battle of wills.

Now, he stood there on this February night in the still-unfinished signature building at 30 Rockefeller Center. All day workers had left their offices. Nelson was armed with his own small army of workers. He told them to remove the canvas from the wall. He gazed at the magnificent mural one last time. He took a deep breath, then gave the order that he was hoping he would not have to give: "Take it down."

The workers climbed on their scaffold and began to chisel the fresco off the wall. Section by section, the mural fell to the marble floor and smashed into pieces. When the last remnant of the mural was removed, the workers swept the debris into large piles, loaded it in containers, and hauled it away from the lobby. Then a new corps of men marched into the building, buckets and trowels in hand, and proceeded to replaster the wall. The destruction was complete. It was as if the magnificent mural had never existed.

When the building was reopened on Monday morning, the tenants couldn't believe what they were looking at in the lobby. Instead of the canvas with its concealed masterpiece waiting to be unveiled, they were met with a gigantic plastered blank wall. The fresco was gone. Reaction was swift. Eleven artists who were scheduled to be part of the Municipal Art Society Exhibition at Rockefeller Center at the end of February refused to display their work to protest the destruction of Rivera's mural. They requested that Rockefeller change the location for the exhibition. They wanted their work to be displayed at a venue not heated in controversy. The head of the American Society of Painters, Sculptors, and Engravers, Leon Kroll, stated, "Regardless of whether it was a great work of art, I don't feel that the Rockefeller family had a moral right to take such action." Protest meetings were planned by Rivera's admirers at the New Workers School on West Fourteenth Street.

Later in February, Diego Rivera himself responded on the loss of his mural. He cabled the following statement from Mexico City:

"The Rockefellers have destroyed my mural, but they cannot prevent me from speaking through my paintings to the workers of New York and the United States. My work was photographed despite the prohibition of the management of Radio City and will be published in permanent form. In destroying my paintings the Rockefellers have committed an act of cultural vandalism. There ought to be, there will yet be, a justice that prevents the assassination of human creation as of human character. The Rockefellers demonstrate that the system they represent is the enemy of human culture, as it is of the further advance of science and the productive powers of mankind."

A short time later, Diego Rivera did replicate his masterpiece fresco, but this time in Mexico City and with a few slight modifications to the original. He placed John D. Rockefeller Jr. in his retooled mural with a microscope above his head. On the microscope there was a slide of the venereal disease syphilis. This was Rivera's final way of expressing how he felt about his mistreatment by the Rockefellers.

Today this version of the mural remains in Mexico City, and Diego Rivera is still regarded as the most acclaimed muralist in the world. The lobby at Rockefeller Center contains a new mural titled "American Progress" by famed Spanish muralist Jose Maria Sert, and is considered one of the finest examples of wall art ever created.

"CLIMB, YOU FOOL"

1945

Saturday morning, July 28, 1945, dawned shrouded in fog. As people were making their way around the city, they occasionally looked up, only to find that the tops of the great skyscrapers were lost in the clouds. A young couple stood alone on the observation deck, trying to be good tourists despite the poor visibility. Everything seemed eerily still. Suddenly, they heard a noise coming from the white mist. It grew louder and louder until it was a deafening roar. The man grabbed his wife and held her tightly against the building. He turned to look out again, and then it happened. His startled reaction was: "I saw this plane, and it looked like it was coming right at me, and the ceiling was zero. I couldn't believe my eyes!" Stanley Lomax, a local radio sports announcer who had just glanced out his office window on Fifth Avenue, realized the impending doom. He shouted in horror, "Climb, you damn fool! Climb!"

The plane hit with such force that the building shook. Flames and debris were shooting out everywhere. The sounds of glass breaking, metal being torn apart, and people screaming could be heard.

The unthinkable had happened: A ten-ton B-25 Mitchell bomber had crashed into the world's tallest structure, the Empire State Building. It was 9:49 a.m. The plane crashed on the seventy-ninth floor, creating a gaping hole eighteen feet wide and twenty feet high. Fuel spilled everywhere, engulfing the building as far down as the seventy-fifth floor. The poor, unfortunate workers coming in on Saturday from the War Relief Services of the National Catholic Welfare Conference received the brunt of the explosion. They had come to work that fateful day to put together care packages for army personnel still stationed overseas. People sitting at their desks were immediately ignited and stairwells became an inferno as some of the terrified workers tried to escape.

When the plane hit, people's imaginations ran wild. World War II was drawing to a close, and some thought that a Japanese kamikaze pilot had crashed into the building in a last show of defiance. Others thought that Hitler, in some twisted way, was exacting revenge from the grave. One woman, Doris Pope, who was in the building at the time, believed that World War II had come to American soil. She remembered, "That day, as we were getting ready to take our office break, we heard this terrible noise, and the building started to shake . . . As we looked out our third-floor window, we saw debris fall onto the street. We immediately thought New York was being bombed."

Others simply could not believe what they were seeing. Helen J. Hurwitt, who had been working in an office across the street, recounted, "My husband and I were in a building directly opposite the Empire State Building . . . Large plate glass windows looked out onto Thirty-fourth Street. The floor we were on was pretty high. At some point, we heard a horrendous noise and rushed to the windows. We were horrified to see a B-25 half in and half out of the Empire State Building."

How could such a tragedy have occurred? Lieutenant Colonel William Smith, who was piloting the U.S. Army B-25 bomber, caught some bad luck as the fog caused him to mistake the route that led to the airport. The plane had been en route from New Bedford, Massachusetts, to New York City. The pilot attempted to make a landing at LaGuardia Airport (along Long Island Sound), but the dense fog had forced him to shift course over Manhattan and possibly attempt a landing at Newark Airport in New Jersey instead. Smith, who was an experienced pilot, West Point graduate, and the recipient of the Army's Distinguished Flying Cross and the Air Medal and France's Croix de Guerre for his wartime service in Europe, made miscalculations trying to cross Manhattan Island.

He tried to use visuals to maintain his location, which caused him to bank left and right to avoid several buildings. There was a report of a plane that had a near miss with the main tower of Rockefeller Center and another with the New York Central Building. There was speculation that Smith may have not known where he was and thought that the East River was actually the Hudson River and headed in that direction. He may never have even seen the Empire State Building looming before him, or if he had, it was probably too late to bank away from it. There is no way anyone will ever know for sure since this was a time prior to "black boxes" on airplanes.

The crash caused severe damage to the building's north side, which was the point of impact. The wings were torn off the plane, and the two engines were dislodged from the body of the aircraft. One engine wound up in an elevator shaft, landing on top of an empty elevator car and sending it plummeting to the basement along with other debris from the plane. Onlookers recounted their firsthand impressions of the event. Catherine O'Connor, who was working in the offices of the War Relief Services, stated, "The plane exploded within the building. There were five or six seconds—I was tottering on my feet trying to keep my balance—and three-quarters of the office was instantaneously consumed in a sheet of flame. One man was standing inside the flame. I could see him. It was a coworker, Joe Fountain. His whole body was on fire. I kept calling to him, 'Come on, Joe; come on, Joe.' He walked out of it."

Meantime, firemen had to face fifteen-foot flames leaping out of the seventy-eighth- and seventy-ninth-floor windows. Equipment had to be taken to the sixtieth floor in order to fight the fire effectively. From there the firemen had to drag the heavy apparatus up and through smoke-filled stairwells to reach the fire's source. Right behind the heroic firemen was the "hands-on mayor," Fiorello LaGuardia. He climbed the sixty floors with the firemen to see if he could be of any assistance putting out the fire or helping survivors. On his heels, of course, was an army of reporters and photographers all wanting to get every juicy detail for the headlines the next day. The fire was declared "under control" after nineteen minutes, and the last flames were extinguished within forty minutes. The blaze had been the highest in New York City history. The city honored the firemen and other volunteer workers at a dedication ceremony held at City Hall weeks later.

One amazing story that came out of this tragedy involved the plane's second engine. It tore through one of the Empire State Building's seventy-three elevator cables and came out the building on the Thirty-third Street side. When the engine severed the cable, the car attached to it also began its descent to the basement. Inside the car was a frightened elevator operator, Betty Lou Oliver. Betty had been injured by flying debris on the eightieth floor and brought to elevator #6 to be "safely" sent down to the lobby for treatment. As the car fell, its rubberized cable began to coil under it, creating a springlike yo-yo effect all the way down. Betty was screaming for her life. Luckily, because of the tight fit of the elevator car in the shaft, air was trapped and helped to cushion the car when it finally hit bottom.

There were several volunteer workers in the lobby of the building, tending to the wounded. One of them, Donald Maloney, heard Betty's screams coming from the elevator shaft. He couldn't believe what he was hearing. Working feverishly to remove the debris and climb into the crushed elevator car, he found her, now unconscious, injured but alive. She had miraculously survived the plunge from the seventy-ninth floor! For many years after, Betty proudly recounted her story of falling one thousand feet and living to tell about it.

But not everyone was so lucky. That day fourteen people lost their lives; three plane crewmen and eleven people in the War Relief Services office. Twenty-five people were also injured, all of whom recovered. Weeks of inquiries followed the crash, and in the end the blame was placed solely on the shoulders of the pilot, Lt. Colonel Smith. Mayor LaGuardia, who had been a flier himself, summed it up the best: "He had one thousand feet of altitude. Traveling at that rate, one thousand feet doesn't last long. This fellow certainly should have been higher."

THE DAY THEY TORE
HISTORY DOWN

1963

It was 9:00 a.m. on a drizzly Monday morning in 1963. The weather reflected the feelings of New Yorkers as the workmen began the destruction, the tearing down of the largest structure of its kind in the world, dominating nine acres of land from Thirty-first Street to Thirty-third Street between Seventh and Eighth Avenues, a huge granite and marble Beaux-Arts building with six three-ton stone eagle statues standing at attention guarding the top of the building. In between the six eagles stood two statues representing Day and Night that leaned against a central clock. The front of the building had eighty-four massive pink Doric columns, each fifty-three feet high and four and a half feet in diameter, that led taxis into a carriageway derived from the Brandenburg gate. Those on foot would stroll through a long, elegant skylight-drenched Italian-style shopping arcade. At the end of the corridor was a waiting room that stretched a block and a half long, with 150-foot-high vaulted ceilings modeled after the imperial Roman bathhouses of Caracalla.

Wrought-iron staircases led down to the trains four stories below. It was designed to represent stability and permanence, and now, just fifty-three years after its opening, it was being demolished at the cost of $116 million.

On Nov. 27, 1910, when Pennsylvania Station opened, it was the first time trains were entering Manhattan by way of tunnels under the Hudson River. Prior to 1910, only one railroad traveled into Manhattan, dropping passengers into Vanderbilt's widely decorated Grand Central Terminal; the other ten existing railroads had to drop their passengers into New Jersey, where a fleet of ferries would then usher the hundreds of thousands of people across the Hudson into Manhattan. Something had to be done to solve this problem. Penn Station was the answer.

Penn Station was the masterpiece of architect Charles McKim from the firm of McKim, Mead, and White. McKim said the building was meant to have "the appearance of a monumental gateway and entrance to one of the great metropolitan cities of the world."

When it opened, over one hundred thousand people and historic greats, such as Babe Ruth and Jack Dempsey, walked through the station. The station was even immortalized in Alfred Hitchcock's 1951 film *Strangers on a Train* when Hitchcock had the star, Farley Granger, chase a murderer through Penn Station at the climax of the movie.

But with all its grandeur, there was still a problem: After fifty-three years the building was run-down and the Pennsylvania Railroad company was nearly in financial ruin due to the competitive increase in air and car travel. The four blocks of property that the building stood on was becoming too valuable a property not to sell. Weighing the odds, the Pennsylvania Railroad signed an agreement with Madison Square Garden (which was then on 49th and Eighth) to build a new sports building complex and demolish the "unnecessary aboveground structure of Penn Station." The actually functional train station below would remain the same. The Penn Station owners claimed "that the city would gain more from the new and offset the 'aesthetic loss.'"

This would be the forth incarnation of Madison Square Garden. MSG would manage and own 75 percent of the building and Pennsylvania Railroad would have a 25 percent interest. The whole deal would have been kept hush-hush, but a *New York Times* article in July 1961 exposed the deal.

The greatest opposition to the developers was the well-coordinated protest campaign organized by architects, artists, and writers. They said buildings like this were what make a city unique and that it should be preserved as an architectural and aesthetic landmark. The *New York Times* and several leading architectural magazines joined the cause. Over the next two years, hundreds marched, wrote letters, took out newspaper ads, and spoke at hearings. That struck a chord with ordinary people, but it hadn't yet caught on with planners and city officials.

Protestors upped the ante. On August 2, 1962, a young group of architects headed by Norval White founded the Action Group for Better Architecture in New York (AGBANY). They were asking the Port Authority to purchase Penn Station and operate it as it did its bridges, tunnels, airports, and seaports. This controversy of old versus new was such a heated battle that it became international news, with slogans like "SHAME" and "Don't Amputate—Renovate."

There was only one big glitch. Protestors had no legal basis to demand Penn Station be maintained since it was a private property, and as long as the developers' plans met with the city zoning laws, there was nothing legally that could be done. The group's hopes laid on a vote by the City Planning Commission, whose approval of a variance was necessary for the project.

Meanwhile the developers launched a counterattack. A pamphlet was put out by the Long Island Railroad called "Inside Penn Station: How to beat the system while we raze the old and raise the new." The pamphlet said, "Watching Penn Station's transformation will be like watching your youngsters growing up—the changes will be taking place day by day, little by little . . . When it's all fixed up, and the contractors have moved out, there'll be: Air conditioning, more escalators, taxis closer to the train gates, more convenient station entrances, new track level ventilating systems, even brighter lighting on all levels, more space on the LIRR concourse, new, more attractive, more convenient stores . . . In short, you'll have one of most modern, spacious, cheerful, and functional terminals in the nation. . . . you're going to like it!"

The battle continued. On May 5, 1963, the architecture critic for the *New York Times,* Ada Louise Huztable, wrote, "If a giant pizza stand were proposed in an area zoned for such usage, and if studies showed acceptable traffic patterns and building densities, the pizza stand would be 'in the public interest,' even if the Parthenon itself stood on the chosen site."

This was an unprecedented display of activism for a preservation cause in New York City. The world waited to see what would happen.

Then the verdict came. In early 1963 the project was approved unanimously by the City Planning Commission.

On that fateful morning of October 28, 1963, there were no protests. Several excited top officials were on the scene including Irving M. Felt, the chairman and president of Madison Square Garden Corporation; Benton Jones, the vice president of Pennsylvania Railroad; and Thomas Goodfellow, the president of Long Island Railroad.

There was a ceremony before the first hammer struck. A giant crane lowered one of the six-ton eagles down to the street. They all took a press photo op with the dethroned eagle.

As the posed smiles faded, the electric jackhammers tore at the granite slabs on the Thirty-third Street side. "This is a sad day for us," said Norman Jaffe, one of the protesting architects. He and others watched wearing black armbands and carrying signs saying, SHAME. But not everyone had the same sentiments. The crew's foreman shrugged his shoulders; to them, "It's just another job."

When questioned about the future of the station's eighty-four Doric columns, a hopeful parks commissioner said he "endorsed a plan to move them to the Battery where they would be put to use."

Unfortunately the columns were transported instead to a landfill in the New Jersey's Meadowlands, where they laid broken, looking like the remains of an ancient Roman temple shattered by an earthquake. One eagle, however, did survive and is held prisoner near Madison Square Garden, south on Seventh Avenue toward Thirty-first Street, fenced in, visited daily by a family of squatter pigeons.

Later the words on the editorial page of the *New York Times* said it best, "Until the First blow, no one was convinced that Penn Station really would be demolished or that New York would permit this monumental act of vandalism . . . we will probably be judged not by the monuments we build but by those we have destroyed." But on that day, all was not lost. The protestors may have lost that battle but won the war.

On April 19, 1965, Mayor Robert Wagner signed the New York City's Landmark Law, which established a Preservation Commission to "safeguard the city's historic, aesthetic, and cultural heritage and foster and enhance civic pride in the beauty and noble accomplishments of the past." This law, which was again upheld in 1978 by the Supreme Court, changed all redevelopment in New York forever.

Since then, the Landmarks Preservation Commission has officially protected 1,100 individual landmarks, including the Empire State Building and Central Park.

Today Penn Station is owned by Amtrak, serving 600,000 passengers a day (compared to 140,000 at Grand Central Terminal). That's a thousand passengers every ninety seconds, the busiest train station in the United States. If you look closely at where some tiles are eroded, glimmers of the old wall still peek through.

A COMIC ON TRIAL

1964

The courtroom was silent on that cold December morning in 1964. The media and spectators waited for the verdict. Thirty-nine-year-old Leonard Alfred Schneider, better known as comic Lenny Bruce, was sitting at the defendant's table alone without counsel. He recently had to dismiss his attorney, Ephraim London, because his own attorney was suing him for legal fees that Bruce couldn't pay since his first arrest on obscenity charges four years ago caused many club owners to cancel his engagements bringing him from earning $350,000 a year down to $5,000. A situation that was not that funny.

You see, Bruce had developed a reputation as an edgy, innovative comedian. Television host Steve Allen introduced him as "the most shocking comedian of our time, a young man who is skyrocketing to fame—Lenny Bruce!" To Bruce nothing was beyond reach; he joked and used four-letter words about Vegas, the Klu Klux Klan, JFK, Dear Abby, sex, race relations, and religion. In one comedy bit called "Religions Inc.," he had prominent church leaders from the Pope to Billy Graham exchanging money-raising tips at company headquarters—a huge no-no back then. Every night the audience would wait with delightful anticipation: "How far will he go tonight?"

The problem was the lawmakers thought he went too far, and this time they weren't joking. It was a double-edged sword. Bruce wanted to keep his audiences happy. As he said to one audience, "Well, you know, we've got a slight problem. If I say the things that you want me to say, those gentlemen back there [vice squad officers attending Bruce's performance] are going to bust me. [Audience boos.] Don't boo them, it's not their fault. They're only doing their job. It's your fault I'm being busted. Until you change the law, they have to do what the law requires them to do. It's up to you to change the law."

But the law wasn't changed soon enough. On April Fool's Day in 1964, four New York City vice squad plainclothes police officers attended Bruce's performance at the Cafe Au Go Go in Greenwich Village. They mingled with the crowd and watched Bruce's act. They were wearing concealed wires. Two nights later, on April 3, right before Bruce's 10:00 p.m. show at the Café Au Go Go, he and the owner, Howard Solomon, were arrested in the dressing room. Assistant District Attorney Richard Kuh presented a grand jury with a typed partial script of Bruce's performance, including references to Jackie Kennedy trying to "save her ass" after her husband's assassination. He posted bail and went back to the club to perform. This time Bruce, the club owner, and the owner's wife were all arrested on April 7.

A few days before the trial started, on June 13, 1964, more than one hundred notables in the community, including actors, musicians, authors, journalists, and scientists such as Richard Burton, Paul Newman, and Elizabeth Taylor, signed a "Petition Protesting the Arrest of Lenny Bruce" and sent it to the press. It started,

"We the undersigned are agreed that the recent arrests of nightclub entertainer Lenny Bruce by the New York police department on charges of indecent performance constitutes a violation of civil liberties as guaranteed by the First and Fourteenth Amendments to the United States Constitution . . . Lenny Bruce is a popular and controversial performer in the field of social satire in the tradition of Swift, Rabelais, and Twain. Although Bruce makes use of the vernacular in his nightclub performances, he does so within the context of his satirical intent and not to arouse the prurient interests of his listeners. It is up to the audience to determine what is offensive to them; it is not a function of the police department of New York or any other city to decide what adult private citizens may or may not hear. Whether we regard Bruce as a moral spokesman or simply as an entertainer, we believe he should be allowed to perform free from censorship or harassment."

But despite the heavy hitters weighing in with their opinion, the trial forged on. You see, this was not Lenny's first arrest.

He had been arrested in Los Angeles and Chicago in 1961 on foul language charges as well, and in both cases he was acquitted for the misdemeanors. He had used the Yiddish word "schmuck." Although the jury had acquitted him, law enforcement agencies began monitoring his comedy appearances, resulting in his arrest several times.

By 1963, with his fame rising, he became the target of Frank Hogan, the Manhattan district attorney, who was close friends with the Archbishop of New York, Francis Cardinal Spellman. Together they claimed that Bruce was the "original comedic Catholic Church basher." Now they had their evidence and they were out for comedic blood.

The trial was postponed for a month due to Bruce being hospitalized with pleurisy.

The media used that time to speak out on his behalf again. After his famed Carnegie Hall show, critic Albert Goldman wrote: "Lenny worshipped the gods of Spontaneity, Candor, and Free Association. He fancied himself an oral jazzman . . . and blow everything that came into his head just as it came into his head with nothing censored, nothing translated, nothing mediated until he was pure mind, pure head sending out brainwaves like radio waves into the heads of every man and woman seated in that vast hall."

Influential San Francisco columnist Herb Caen wrote, "They call Lenny Bruce a sick comic, and sick he is. Sick of all the pretentious phoniness of a generation that makes his vicious humor meaningful. He is a rebel, but not without a cause, for there are shirts that need un-stuffing, egos that need deflating. Sometimes you feel guilty laughing at some of Lenny's mordant jabs, but that disappears a second later when your inner voice tells you with pleased surprise, 'but that's true.'"

On June 20, 1964, when the trial finally began, the defense moved to dismiss the prosecution against Bruce on constitutional grounds. But the case still proceeded.

During the trial the defense called a parade of eighteen celebrity witnesses to prove Bruce's act had significant redeeming social value. Woody Allen, Bob Dylan, Jules Feiffer, Allen Ginsberg, Norman Mailer, William Styron, and James Baldwin, among other artists, writers, and educators, as well as Manhattan journalist and television personality Dorothy Kilgallen and sociologist Herbert Gans and even a minister spoke.

The prosecution called their witnesses as well. Herbert S. Rune, an NYC department of licenses inspector, said he had jotted down notes during Bruce's performance. He read language used out of context, just highlighting the curse words. Both patrolmen who were at the club on April 1st gave similar testimony. The hidden wire tape used in court was scratchy and hissy and barely audible, but Inspector Rune jumped in and offered damaging substitutions, just based on some jotted down notes he had written when watching Bruce's act. The defense attorney objected, but the damage was done.

During the trial, Hugh Hefner, a man who hated censorship himself, approached Bruce. Hugh convinced Bruce to write his autobiography, which was serialized in *Playboy* in 1964 and 1965; it was later published into a book, *How to Talk Dirty and Influence People.*

Now after six months of testimony, they waited for the decision. If convicted, Bruce's words would land him in jail for up to a year. He and Mr. and Mrs. Howard Solomon sat quietly as the three-judge panel consisting of Judge Randall Creel, Judge John Murtagh, and Judge Kenneth Phipps were about to render their decision, a decision that would be unlike any ever before handed down in a court of law in New York. There never had been a previous case in New York where a performer was charged with obscenity on the basis of his words alone; the laws governing obscenity were too vague and open to mass interpretation. The prosecuting attorney, Assistant District Attorney Kuh, was sitting confidently.

On December 21, 1964, Lenny Bruce was found guilty by a two-to-one vote on obscenity charges. He was sentenced to four months in a workhouse even though this was just a misdemeanor charge. The club owner was sentenced to six months in jail or a $1,000 fine. His wife was found not guilty.

Two judges found him guilty, saying his performances were "obscene, indecent, immoral, and impure." The third judge, Creel, disagreed: "in a total absence of any guideposts or other directives from such higher courts I fear we proceeded not unlike an explorer plunged into a vast uncharted virgin area in pursuit of a mirage or some fabled lost golden city. In this quest the time-honored rules of evidence proved to be something of a highly unsuitable encumbrance, and the judicial process revealed itself as a most limited and inadequate, if not improper, tool for this task."

Bruce was set free on bail during the appeals process, but the damage was done. For years now he had performed, pleased the crowds, and been arrested. It was a vicious circle, and it took its toll, trial by trial, dollar by dollar, year after year.

He gave his last performance on June 25, 1966, at the Fillmore Auditorium in San Francisco. Billy Graham criticized his performance. By then Bruce had been blacklisted by almost every club in the country because the owners feared they would be prosecuted along with him for allowing the obscenities. Depressed and bankrupt, having to give up the very thing he loved, he turned to heavy drugs.

On August 3, 1966, Lenny was found dead on the bathroom floor in his Hollywood Hills home, due to morphine overdose. At the funeral five hundred people paid their respects. Dick Schaap famously eulogized Bruce in *Playboy,* with the memorable last line: "One last four-letter word for Lenny: Dead. At forty. That's obscene."

Bruce died before the appeal was decided. After Bruce's death, one of his New York prosecutors, Assistant District Attorney Vincent Cuccia, expressed regret over his role:

> *I feel terrible about Bruce. We drove him into poverty*
> *and bankruptcy and then murdered him. I watched*
> *him gradually fall apart. It's the only thing I did in*
> *Hogan's office that I'm really ashamed of. We all knew*
> *what we were doing. We used the law to kill him.*

Solomon's conviction was eventually overturned by New York's highest court, the New York Court of Appeals, in 1970.

Bruce became a comedy legend. After his death, plays, documentaries, and books were written. John Lennon, Bob Dylan, REM,

Simon and Garfunkel, and hundreds of others referred to him in their songs. (Steve Earle wrote "F the CC," which includes the lyric "Dirty Lenny died so we could all be free.") Bruce also influenced pop culture; his one attempt to be released from the military in WWII by dressing in women's clothes was said to be the inspiration for the Klinger character in *M*A*S*H**, and the phrase "Yadda yadda yadda," made famous in a *Seinfeld* episode, was originally in a Lenny Bruce routine called "Father Flotski's Triumph." Bruce even had a memorial beer named after him called Bittersweet Lenny's RIPA. And in 2004 Bruce was voted number three of the one hundred greatest comics of all time by Comedy Central, coming in behind Richard Pryor and George Carlin.

On December 23, 2003, Lenny Bruce made history again. New York Governor George Pataki, upon a petition that was signed by several stars such as Robin Williams, granted Bruce the first posthumous pardon in the state's history. Pataki said it was a "declaration of New York's commitment to upholding the First Amendment."

Comedy greats like George Carlin, Richard Pryor, Robin Williams, and Chris Rock all say their comedy could have never existed if Lenny Bruce had not torn down the conventional walls of comedy.

LILLIPUTIAN NEW YORK

1964

It was April 22, 1964. A black limousine rolled up to the entrance of the New York City Pavilion, and a hulking man in a long gabardine trench coat stepped out. The man, who never needed to learn to drive, looked around as thousands of people applauded. He acknowledged the crowd with a nod of his head, leaned over to the chauffeur, barked out some orders in a deep raspy voice, and walked majestically toward the entrance of the building as if the world was his to command. The man was Robert Moses, Parks Commissioner of the Greater City of New York.

Moses entered the lobby of the New York City Building, and every eye was on him. There was an air of seriousness in his demeanor and a look of concern on his face. He was about to unveil his masterpiece. A masterpiece that had taken over one hundred people three years to complete. Moses was assured that every effort was made to guarantee the accuracy of this Lilliputian project (making persons and things of very small size). He needed this to be done right and had demanded that there be a margin of error of only 1

percent. The contractors knew if they didn't come through and violated the agreement in any way, they wouldn't get their money. This
was the largest scale model ever assembled. It consisted of 895,000
buildings and 273 rectangular blocks, representing an exact replica of
his beloved city. He called it *The Panorama of the City of New York*.
Moses had planned this as a major part of his last hurrah, and he was
going to display it at the spectacular 1964 World's Fair in Flushing
Meadows, Queens.

Robert Moses was known as "The Power Broker." He had been
in control of various New York City agencies for more than forty
years. He was one of the greatest innovators of New York City transportation and population dispersion because he had built a great
number of bridges, tunnels, highways, and parks created under his
regime. Almost single-handedly, he united the five boroughs of New
York with the suburbs of Long Island, Westchester County, Rock-
land County, Connecticut, and New Jersey with his achievements,
which also served as monuments to the city's success.

But a man like this is often outspoken. He would cut down
any who opposed him with statements like, "Those who can, build.
Those who can't, criticize." This *Panorama* was a fantastic way for
the world to get a glimpse of all his achievements at one time, something that greatly appealed to his enormous ego.

Moses decided that the *Panorama* should not just be another
exhibition at the World's Fair that would be taken down at the end
of the year. He needed it to be a more permanent structure, a last-
ing monument to his work. To ensure this, the contract for building
the *Panorama* stated, "The complete model should be designed as a
comprehensive planning and study device for use after the closing of
the World's Fair." Moses decided that he would put the model in the
New York City Pavilion, a building that already existed in Flushing
Meadow Park. The Pavilion had been preserved from the original

1939 World's Fair and was actually the site of the United Nations beginning in 1946, prior to the move to its permanent location on First Avenue in Manhattan. The U.N. continued to meet in Flushing Meadows for four years and voted on such important resolutions as the forming of the State of Israel and the creation of UNICEF there. The U.N.'s stay helped pay for the upkeep of Flushing Meadow Park. It also opened the door for the 1964 World's Fair site to be in this location. At the moment, the building was being used as a skating rink and had the sufficient space not only to handle the *Panorama* but also to accommodate the hundreds of people Moses hoped would be visiting it on a daily basis.

To take on this behemoth project, "The Power Broker" hired the architectural firm of Raymond Lester and Associates. The architects decided to build the *Panorama* in sections, off-site, and then to assemble it on-site, elevated above the floor of the pavilion, which would allow for adjustments and repairs to be made. To make sure this project was perfect, they consulted many maps compiled from a variety of sources before they even began any of the construction. Once the plans were finalized, the workers were assembled. The workers had the task of making this dream a reality. They had to build the model out of wood, plastic, flakeboard, and urethane foam sheets. They knew they were creating something very special and took great pains to ensure that the buildings, all built on a scale of one inch to one hundred feet, were in perfect proportion to each other and to the land that it occupied. For example, the Empire State Building was fifteen inches high, the Bronx Zoo covered fifteen hundred square inches, and the Staten Island Ferry traveled twenty-two feet across New York Harbor.

During the entire three years of construction, Robert Moses watched the project with a keen eye. This was part of his legacy and everything had to be done right. He was often seen walking through the model looking at the details and checking underneath to make sure it was sturdy. Moses also had something else to consider. How was he going to make sure that all the visitors to the World's Fair would get to view his legacy? His model had to compete with the great exhibitions created by the giants of industry. Moses came up with the answer. Using help from a magician named Walt Disney, he decided people shouldn't walk around the *Panorama*—they should "fly" over it, just like an amusement park ride.

When visitors would walk into the Pavilion, they waited in line, paid a dime, and entered a small car that moved along a track. They would hear newscaster Lowell Thomas utter, "Let's get ready for a take-off flight into the past and present of the Greatest City on Earth." The ride tracked above the city and traveled the full length of the five boroughs. Along the way, Lowell Thomas pointed out many of New York City's greatest landmarks. A tiny plane on wires descended into LaGuardia Airport every minute, and the skies darkened periodically to reflect the changes in time, as Lowell Thomas continued his commentary with such glowing words as, "Center of civilization, this electric metropolis has opened opportunity to all, and its reward has been greatness." By using this feature of a nine-minute simulated helicopter ride around the city, Moses hoped that this would be one of the most successful attractions at the Fair. It was also a great way to control how long people would linger at the exhibit: the quicker the line moved, the more people who could pay and see it. Moses was always thinking what was best for business.

When Robert Moses walked through the doors of the New York City Pavilion on that morning in April, a big smile crossed his face. It was not very often that his associates saw this side of him. Moses strolled past the replica of New Amsterdam as it appeared in 1660, a model that was purposely put there to be in sharp contrast to the *Panorama of New York* they were about to experience. He walked directly to the model, looked carefully over the expanse, and made sure that all was in order. This project had cost the city under $700,000, but he felt it was worth it. He welcomed the press and dignitaries who had assembled from all over the world for the opening ceremonies of the 1964 World's Fair. Being a man of few words, Robert Moses made a few general remarks. He knew that this work would speak for itself. It would bring him all the accolades he craved. With a wave of his hand Robert Moses ushered the crowd in to view New York City as they had never seen it before. As expected, they loved the model.

Unfortunately, the 1964 World's Fair itself was never the complete success that Robert Moses hoped it would be. However, his dream that the *Panorama* would live on came true. The *Panorama*, today, resides at its original World's Fair location, Flushing Meadows Corona Park. It is no longer called the New York City Pavilion but is now the Queens Museum of the Arts, where over one hundred thousand visitors a year view this splendid artistic achievement. Gone is the simulated helicopter ride. It has been replaced by a giant ramp that rims the entire perimeter. Visitors now have the opportunity to speak to docents firsthand and find out everything they can about the construction of this great model.

The *Panorama* was updated in 1970 and 1992, at a cost of $1 million, so that architects could change over sixty thousand structures to reflect the changes in the New York City skyline. Plans are now in the works for another update, which will result in more than another eighty thousand buildings being either erected or removed to reflect the enormous change that New York City has undergone in the past few years. When visitors come to view the *Panorama* today, the thing that strikes most people is that on the southern tip of Manhattan the Twin Towers still stand proudly.

THE GANGSTER CELEBRITY

1972

Joey Gallo sat with his back to the door in Umberto's Clam House at 129 Mulberry Street in the Little Italy section of New York City. His sharply tailored suit made him look quite dapper as he reclined in his chair at the butcher block table, enjoying Italian delicacies and slowly drinking his soda. It was 4:00 a.m., Friday morning, April 7, 1972. Gallo was with his new bride of three weeks, Sina; his ten-year-old daughter from his prior marriage; and his bodyguard, Pete the Greek who had brought his date, even though he was married with a family.

Gallo and his party had just come from his forty-third birthday bash celebration hosted by Broadway actor Jerry Orbach, comedian David Steinberg, and columnist Earl Wilson at the famed Copacabana nightclub in midtown New York. They had decided to grab a late-night supper before heading home. They weren't sure which restaurant would be open at that hour but found Umberto's still had its lights on. They decided that this would be the place. It had good food, simply cooked the old-fashioned Italian way. Little did the group know, but they were being watched by Joey Luparelli, a driver and bodyguard for Gallo's arch enemy, Joseph Colombo, another crime boss. He quickly headed down the street. This was his chance to make points with his boss. Luparelli found Carmine DiBiase, also an associate of Colombo, and two brothers he only knew as Cisco and Benny. They spoke briefly, agreed to meet a few minutes later in front of Umberto's, and then went to get their weapons.

Five other patrons were dining in at Umberto's that night, as was Matty the Horse, a frequent visitor to the restaurant and a mob-connected club owner. Suddenly, the front door burst open and the three men entered with their .38s blazing. Gallo stood up and immediately was hit in the chest. He knew that he was the intended target of the hit and didn't want innocent people caught in the cross fire. Gallo staggered forward toward the front door, in an effort to draw the fire, and was struck with several more rounds. Meanwhile, Pete the Greek drew his gun, tried to stand, but was forced to dive to the floor after he was hit with a bullet in the thigh. Screaming could be heard all over Mulberry Street as the other terrified diners hid under tables and behind counters.

Gallo made it as far as the street and then collapsed face first with a thud, breaking his nose in the process. Pete the Greek finally was able to get to his feet and pushed open the back door, where he saw a car with the motor running and began to fire. He managed to get off seven shots, hitting the car several times, but it was too late; the gangsters sped off into the night. The bodyguard dragged himself to the street where Gallo lay in a pool of blood. Pete the Greek knew that he had not done his job. His boss and friend was dead. Thus the life of one of the most colorful Mafia characters of all time came to an abrupt end, literally going out with a bang on his birthday.

Mafia hits are not uncommon, but Joey Gallo was not your common Mafia chief. He was nicknamed "Crazy" by his enemies for his recklessness as a hit man. Gallo was probably responsible for the barbershop hit on mob boss Albert Anastasia, but his guilt was never proven. However, Gallo also had an intellectual and humanitarian side, as well as a great thirst for knowledge. During his numerous prison stays, especially the one at the Auburn Correctional Facility, he developed his intellectual side by reading as many books as possible. He avidly read the works of such great authors as Franz Kafka, Jean-Paul Sartre, Alexander Dumas, Victor Hugo, Leo Tolstoy, and Ayn Rand. Daily, he devoured every word of the *New York Times.* Gallo considered Niccolo Machiavelli to be his role model, and his philosophy was, "No matter what you do in life, be the best. Whether it be a cab driver or a gangster, don't be second rate." You might say that "Crazy Joe" was an intellectual killer. He was described by his friends as "articulate with excellent verbal skills." He could describe gouging out a man's guts with the same eloquence that he used when describing classical literature. This level of sophistication allowed him to mingle with members of high society in New York and with many people in the theater arts. Quite a contrast for a man engaged in such a violent profession.

Gallo's introduction to the theater arts came about in a rather unusual way. During one of his stints in jail, Gallo read about a movie based on the novel by Jimmy Breslin, *The Gang that Couldn't Shoot Straight.* The movie was about a Brooklyn Mafia tribe that, very coincidentally, resembled his gang. Gallo found none of the similarities very flattering or amusing. One of those unmistakable similarities was that the gang leader possessed a pet lion that he kept in his basement. In reality, Joey Gallo had a pet lion in the basement of his Brooklyn apartment on President Street. The lion was used as a scare tactic in his many extortion schemes and as a threat when he went after clients who owed the loan shark money.

After Gallo's release from prison, he called Jerry Orbach and requested a meeting. Unfortunately for Orbach, he was the actor who played the "Crazy Joe-like" character called "Kid Sally" in the movie *The Gang that Couldn't Shoot Straight*. Joey Gallo did not appreciate the actor's depiction of him and wanted to pay him a visit to express his opinion.

Orbach thought that this was it: the end of his acting career and his life. He saw no way out. Orbach agreed to meet with Gallo and "discuss" his portrayal. During their meeting, Orbach and Gallo discovered that they were strikingly similar and soon became the best of friends. This friendship led to Gallo's association with the theatrical elite of New York and Hollywood.

Gallo had also developed a strong relationship with the African-American community, especially its youth, in the 1960s. His idea was to unite the underworld forces of both the Italians and the blacks. This relationship blossomed while he was incarcerated. When he was released in 1971, Gallo predicted a shift in power from the Italian Mafia to African-American gangs, concerning illegal pursuits in the Harlem area. He decided to start his own private war against the Colombo crime family so he could have the power. Gallo took on allies and joined with Carlo Gambino's gang to fight Colombo. On the night of June 28, 1971, Joe Colombo was shot by Jerome Johnson, an African-American member of a Harlem gang and a known associate of Gallo's. Immediately after the hit, Johnson was shot by Colombo bodyguards. The incident proved to Gallo that he was right about his idea of the power shift in Harlem and the necessity of aligning himself with the black community. But it may have been the reason that he became the target for a mob hit. No one messed with "the family" and lived to tell about it.

But "Crazy Joe" Gallo's story did not end with his death on a New York street. The local parish priest refused to provide him a proper Catholic funeral, and Gallo's widow was forced to bring in a priest all the way from Cleveland to preside over the ceremony.

Before the casket was lowered in the ground at Greenwood Cemetery in Brooklyn, Joey's sister, Carmella, threw herself on her brother's coffin. She screamed for all those assembled to hear, "The streets are going to run with blood, Joey!" Her words rang true as an all-out gang war exploded among the Mafia families of New York.

Ironically, no one was ever prosecuted for the murder of "Crazy Joe" Gallo, even though most of the evidence did point to DiBiase, Cisco, and Benny. Joe Luparelli, who had turned government snitch, even testified to the guilt of the three men, but to no avail. However, the story does not end here, either. In 2003 a union activist turned hit man named Frank Sheeran gave several deathbed confessions regarding unsolved crimes in the New York metropolitan area. In one of those confessions, Sheeran swore that he, and he alone, killed Joey Gallo on that April night in 1972. The authorities listened but again took no action. To this day "Crazy Joe" Gallo's murder remains an unsolved crime in the files of the New York City Police Department.

THE BULL ON WALL STREET

1989

As Billy Crystal once said, "It took me twenty years to become an overnight success." However, some artists do it in a statement that is so passionate and bold that it causes an overnight sensation. Such was the case with Italian-American artist Arturo Di Modica.

Arturo was born in Vittoria, Sicily, in the province of Ragusa on January 26, 1941. At a young age he was drawn to art, and by the time he was nineteen, he felt sculpting was his calling, so he left his family and headed for Florence to enroll in the Academia Del Nudo Libero to be amongst talented and aspiring artists. That was in 1960. After just two years he opened his first studio in Florence and developed an impressive following of his bronze and metal works, winning numerous awards. By 1973, he opened a studio in New York City in Soho.

Shortly after the financial crash of 1987, Arturo wanted to find a way to use his creative talents to come up with a symbol that would inspire and represent the "strength and power of the American people." After much thinking he came up with the idea of donating a huge gift.

He realized that on Wall Street there are two markets, the bull and the bear. A bull market is associated with increasing investor confidence, and because of that optimism, investors buy in anticipation of future price increases and future capital gains. A large group of these bull participants is called the herd doing a bull run.

A bear market, however, is the opposite, in which investors are pessimistic; anticipating losses, they are motivated to sell stocks, with the negative feeling creating a downward vicious cycle, such as in the Wall Street crash of 1929, the 1970s energy crisis, the 1987 stock market crash, and the most recent financial crisis from 2007–2009. Prices fluctuate on Wall Street all the time, but to make it a bear market, there has to be a price decline of 20 percent or more over at least a two-month period.

With that in mind, in two years Arturo created a black patina bronze and stainless steel running bull statue. Using $360,000 of his own money, Arturo designed a mold in a local Brooklyn foundry. After months of pouring the 2,500-degree metals, he had the pieces he needed. They were carefully transported to his studio, where, one by one, the pieces of a gigantic bull were welded together under his supervision.

The week of December 15, 1989, Arturo decided to do some undercover work. He stood outside the New York Stock Exchange (NYSE) and observed the movements of the guards. He timed their breaks, and noted how many guards were around and how tight security was late at night. After noting everything carefully, his surveillance was done and a date was set for the silent unveiling.

Arturo then rented a crane and a flatbed truck with a hoist arm attached. He carefully roped and cloaked his long-horned, pavement-pawing, snorting behemoth. All of the sixteen-foot-wide, eleven-foot-high, three-and-half-ton bronze beauty was covered in tarps.

Then with the help of thirty of his friends, at the wee hour of 1:00 a.m. on Friday, December 15, 1989, Arturo and his artsy gang drove to the New York Stock Exchange. The streets were deserted. As he pulled around the corner, ready to drop the bull and run, he got a surprise himself. There, on the yellow centerline of Broad Street where he planned to place the bull, stood a huge sixty-foot Christmas tree. Apparently a lot of people like to place things in the middle of the night. Deciding in an instant that his Yuletide gift would fit perfectly under the tree, Arturo instructed his gang to silently lower the bull. Swiftly, like a pack of elves, the deed was done in five minutes flat. The bull was left looking like he was pulling the huge tree and charging toward Wall Street and Federal Hall. Arturo was pleased.

The next morning the media had a field day. Flyers titled "The Bull by Arturo Di Modica" were handed out. The pamphlet started, "The Stock Market crash of 1987 was for many Americans an event frightening in its implications. . . . the artist was inspired to create a monumental work attesting to the vitality, energy, and life of the American people in adversity . . ." It was basically a full-page ode to his work and signed by him. Radio, television, and newspapers all talked about the bull that magically appeared. Curiosity seekers came in droves to see this massive artwork. Throngs snapped photos, others petted the bull, still others thought it was a sign from God and reminiscent of the golden calf from biblical days. The crowd loved it, the stock exchange workers loved it, and many people called the exchange to request that they leave the bull under the tree. Meanwhile reporters were scrambling around trying to get interviews with Arturo.

However, not everyone was pleased. Head honchos and government officials do not like surprises, especially when tons of paperwork and permits are necessary. The NYSE CEO, Richard Grasso, was not happy with the "unauthorized" figure under "their" tree and in front of the exchange. The security officials at the exchange were not happy either; how could this happen under their guard? So they called the police. As one officer, Joseph Gallagher, put it, "In effect they told us there was a very large statue of a bull there, and it wasn't there yesterday, and to the best of their knowledge it shouldn't be there." Police came down but decided it wasn't their problem to foot the bill for removal of the bull.

As the police were deciding what should be done with the bull with no permit, the exchange took things into their own hands, and by the end of the day, they hired a Queens trucking company to cart "The Beastie" away, claiming they "were concerned about safety, security, and public access." After all, "that's a very busy thoroughfare."

Meanwhile, reporters were busy tracking down Arturo and getting quotes from his assistant, Kim Stippa, as to why Arturo just didn't get approval for his work. She later told police, "He had a negative reaction in the past and decided not to apply for a permit."

By the end of the workday, the bull wound up in a holding pen in Queens at the cost of $5,000 to the stock exchange for its removal, and the Dow Jones industrial average was down 14.08 points. Arturo was deeply saddened his bull had been removed, and those on Wall Street were a little worried the removal might be responsible for the downslide.

The next day the headlines in the *New York Post* read, "BAH, HUMBUG! New York Stock Exchange grinches can't bear Christmas gift bull."

To salvage the gift, a senior official, Jill Mainelli, from the NYC Parks department called The Bowling Green Association on lower Broadway and suggested the bull might look great at Bowling Green. After some sizing up of the statue, a representative of the association agreed.

Arturo was called, and arrangements were made for him to see the alternative spot for the bull that night. Arturo decided his masterpiece would fit nicely there.

There were a few minor details, however, to attend to. First, Arturo had to see if he could get his bull back. The NYSE agreed to let their prisoner go to the tune of the $5,000 they had to pay to cart it away. Arturo paid.

Second, permission was needed from the city to place the bull in Bowling Green. A call was placed to NYC parks commissioner, Henry Stern, who was an art and animal lover. Henry in turn called Mayor Edward Koch for a weekend approval. With a quick cut through red tape, the bull now had a permit and was due to arrive at its new home on Wednesday, December 20.

The last thing needed was a name for the bull. Arturo named it "Charging Bull."

On that Wednesday at noontime, the streets were closed and Commissioner Stern led a very joyful ceremony welcoming Charging Bull to Bowling Green. This time Arturo carefully guided the bull to its new home facing up Broadway in the light of day. Ironically it was placed before a large Christmas tree in Bowling Square; this time, however, the city thanked Arturo for his gift. It was quite a turn of events. The bull was an immediate sensation.

The bull still stands in that very spot twenty years later. It has been called by many names: "Christmas Bull," "Italian Bull," "Wall Street Bull," and "Bowling Green Bull." It has come to symbolize many things, especially optimism and prosperity, and is often photographed and rubbed for good luck, so much so that parts of it (nose, horns, and organs) brightly gleam. It is known throughout the world and is visited by tourists just as much as the Statue of Liberty and Empire State Building.

Over the years many things have happened with the statue: On the fifteenth anniversary of the placing of the bull (December 20, 2004), Arturo put the bull up for auction to the highest bidder, "providing that the new owner must leave the bull where it is and donate it to the City of New York." There have been some bidders but they have not met with a price Arturo is happy with as of yet. Arturo's bull even garnered him one of the most prestigious U.S. awards, the Ellis Island Medal of Honor.

In September of 2006 Arturo filed a lawsuit against several corporations, including Walmart, for incorporating images of the bull in their advertising without permission.

In 2008 some people actually knelt down and prayed to the Charging Bull for God to intercede in the market.

As for Arturo, he is now on to even bigger things. He is building a studio complex in Sicily; working on models of ninety-foot horses in his hometown of Ragua, which when finished will be the largest statues in all of Europe; and is commissioned to design a grand fountain for New York City.

ONE INCH PER MINUTE

1998

Seven point four million pounds! The massive building sat mounted on steel rollers under piston units that would slowly roll it down Forty-second Street, from close to Seventh Avenue to a new location almost at Eighth Avenue. It was only a move of one hundred and seventy feet down the block, but every precaution had to be in place. There was the constant threat of the possible failure of such an endeavor; in December the old Selwyn Theater, just across the street, had collapsed during renovations. The plan was to move the building at the pains-takingly slow rate of one inch per minute. The Urban Foundations/Engineer workers who were in charge of the actual physical moving of this landmark building, at a cost of $1.2 million or, in other terms, about $589 per inch, held their collective breaths as the first whish of the pistons and the groan of the ball bearings began. Then, slowly but surely, the steel rollers began to turn, pulling the massive theater along the block, inch by inch. Engineers kept a careful eye to make sure that the structural integrity remained intact. With every foot, they checked to make sure that the ball bearings moved flawlessly and the building was not undergoing any stress. It took patience. After all, this was no young structure. It was an eighty-six-year-old theater that needed to be handled with loving care so it could make it safely to its new home.

Thousands of people lined the streets and were craning their necks to see this mammoth undertaking. Despite the chill in the air, many of them had arrived early in the morning to witness the spectacle. They stood bundled in layers of clothing, holding cups of coffee and hot chocolate, not knowing quite what to expect. Then the building began to move. Immediately, the crowd was warmed by the sight of two giant balloons, representing the comedy team of Abbot and Costello, in front of the procession. It seemed as if the balloons were pulling the massive structure slowly down the street. The symbolism was perfect. This renowned comedy team had performed here for the first time more than sixty years before.

It was March 1, 1998, and the famed Empire Theater was being pushed west down Forty-second Street, toward the Port Authority Bus Terminal, to make way for a $160 million, 335,000-square-foot retail and entertainment complex. It was the first step toward fixing up the seedy area, a nine-hundred-foot-long block of Forty-second Street between Broadway and Eighth Avenue. This was the beginning of the rejuvenation.

The area close to the Eighth Avenue Port Authority Bus Terminal was known as "the Minnesota Strip." It was where young girls from all over the country would be picked up or abducted by pimps and turned toward a world of sex, vice, and corruption. For many years, this part of Forty-second Street had the reputation of being one of the worst and most unsafe places in New York City. The street was lined with porno shops, nude peep shows, streetwalkers, prostitutes, and drug dealers. If you drove down the street, people were at your car window in a second badgering you to engage in some illegal act.

New York City wanted to clean up this street by transforming it into a safe, family-friendly area that promoters had dubbed the "New Forty-second Street."

What started all this? This chain reaction was caused by the advent of the Disney Corporation's renovation of the New Amsterdam Theater on that street. This venture had been under way since 1980, when both the City of New York and the State of New York sanctioned the creation of the Street Development Project. It was not until 1990, however, that things really started to get off the ground when the new 42nd Street Development Project approached major corporations with incentives to build on the street, and in 1993, when Disney agreed to take ownership of the New Amsterdam, the block actually began to experience major physical changes. Major corporations and G-rated entertainment providers got on the "New Forty-second Street" bandwagon and began to replace the corrupt, seedy, and sexually perverse establishments with their own family-oriented venues. Companies like McDonald's, Hilton Hotels, Loews Movie Theaters, Ford Motors, and American Airlines, along with Madame Tussaud's Wax Museum, Ripley's Believe It or Not, B. B. King's Restaurant, Chevy's Restaurant, and others, joined Disney and the Ratner Corporation to make this dream happen.

However, there was one thing that was out of place in the scheme of things: the old Empire Theater! To make this work, they needed to either tear the building down or move it to make room for the new venues.

But in New York City, every street, every building has a story. In the late 1800s this, the area once known as Longacre Square, was the center for horse and carriage commerce. It was mostly the property of the Astor family. John Jacob Astor, one of New York's wealthiest men, often quoted that his biggest regret was that he didn't buy *all* of Manhattan Island when he anticipated and saw the growth of the city northward. In 1901 the *New York Times* moved uptown to this new and developing area. In honor of their new location and shiny new office tower, the company decided to celebrate New Year's Eve in an "explosive" manner with the ball dropping on Times Square! As they say, the rest is history, and on New Year's Eve, a huge turn-out continue this tradition.

By the turn of the century and the early 1900s, Forty-second Street was lined with theaters for the growing population of the city, who were looking for entertainment and excitement. The Eltinge Theater (later renamed the Empire Theater) was a landmark in those days of vaudeville, and it featured a unique act. By day Julian Eltinge was a hard-fisted, aggressive, "manly" man, and by night he was a stage performer who had enough "star quality" persona to have a theater named after him. But what did he do to warrant such an honor? Julian Eltinge was the greatest female impersonator of his time, accepted in the early 1900s as a legitimate act. Onstage, Eltinge received great success and notoriety for his performances. He appeared on the vaudeville circuit and toured Europe before kings and nobility. His convincing portrayal of women led people to brand him "Mr. Lillian Russell." Offstage, he wanted to rid people of the notion that he was homosexual. So he was overly aggressive and engaged in bar brawls, incessant cigar smoking, long engage-ments (but he never married), and fisticuffs with the stagehands. Once asked if he was gay, Eltinge responded, "No, I just like pearls!" His male overcompensation backfired because it made people think he was actually gay. No one really knows and to this day it remains a mystery.

The Eltinge Theater had seen many historic and momentous performances. Sir Laurence Olivier made his American debut in a performance of *Murder on the Second Floor* in 1929. Jackie Gleason, whose statue of "Ralph Kramden" stands conspicuously in front of the Port Authority business station entrance (remember, Ralph was a bus driver), got his start at the Eltinge Burlesque Show as the wisecracking joke teller who introduced the strippers and comedy acts. In 1936 Bud Abbot and Lou Costello first performed onstage. Ironically, both men had performed with other partners and were not very successful. After working together at the Eltinge, they decided to attempt a comedy team partnership that led to them being in over thirty movies and on multiple radio broadcasts and television appearances.

The Eltinge Theater was shut down in 1942 by Mayor Fiorello LaGuardia in an effort to clean up the risqué aura that surrounded Times Square. The Eltinge reopened a short time later as the Empire Theater, a movie house instead of a theater. By 1980, the Empire Theater finally closed its doors due to economic bad times that New York City was going through and the vice that had taken over Forty-second Street.

But even with all that history, that's not why the fabulous building was spared demolition. It was a designated landmark, and so destruction was out of the question. Now it was the job of the The Forest City Ratner Corporation, led by entrepreneur developer and chief executive Bruce Ratner, to ensure no damage would come to the 1912 theater during its move. And in doing so, they were also protecting their $160 million investment to change the neighborhood.

On that March day in 1998, the Empire Theater started its new life but in a slightly different location. After many hours of trepidation by the engineers, and with much fanfare on the part of the cheering spectators and the hoards of press who had assembled for the occasion, the theater reached its destination unscathed. The engineers let out a collective sigh of relief as the theater was set down on its new foundation.

Today, the Empire Theater still stands proudly on Forty-second Street as the entrance to the AMC Empire 25 Movie Complex (so aptly named!). The grandeur of the beautiful historic lobby still remains, but now it is filled with ticket booths, concession stands, and multiple escalators leading to the twenty-five separate theaters. Long gone is the single stage that epitomized the glorious days of vaudeville and burlesque in New York City, but to her credit the Big Apple did find a way to preserve the past for future generations.

A MIRACLE, A GHOST,
AND GEORGE WASHINGTON

2001

The sky was darkened with dust and smoke billowing from the Twin Towers. The ground shook as the massive structures, standing over 1,200 feet high, began to crumble. Debris spewed everywhere as, one by one, they fell. Across the street, approximately two hundred yards west of the disintegrating Towers, was the World Financial Center with its signature atrium, the beautiful glass-domed Winter Garden. To the east of the Towers, approximately the same distance, sat a diminutive church built in 1766.

As horrified onlookers gazed at the sight of the collapse of the Twin Towers and the destruction of the Winter Garden, many of them wondered whether a similar fate would befall the oldest existing church in New York City, a church where George Washington worshipped as President of the United States. But on that tragic day of September 11, 2001, a date that no one will ever forget, a miracle happened. As the Towers fell, clouds of smoke and ash billowed up, totally obstructing the view of the area. As things began to settle down, astonished witnesses couldn't believe their eyes. There was little St. Paul's Church still standing, without the slightest bit of damage except for a toppled lone sycamore tree that landed in the graveyard and piles of ash strewn everywhere. It was a miracle.

But it was not the first time that St. Paul's Church had been blessed. The church can be described as "the little church that stood." It was built in 1766 during a time when the population of Manhattan Island was moving northward. Trinity Church, the seat of the Episcopal Church in New York City, at the intersection of Broadway and Wall Street, eight blocks to the south, was becoming overcrowded with worshippers. To accommodate the growing number of congregants, the board of Trinity Church decided to build an auxiliary facility in which the overflow crowd could attend services. For ten years, St. Paul's held this group of worshippers.

By the fall of 1776, the American Revolution was in full swing, George Washington was forced to flee from Brooklyn and seek refuge in Harlem, and Lord William Howe's British forces were firmly entrenched in the city. Then on the evening of September 21, 1776, a great fire broke out in lower Manhattan. No one is sure how the fire started, but most people, including Washington himself, speculated that it was deliberately set by Patriots who wanted to prevent the British from having comfortable quarters and the necessities they needed while occupying the city. Whatever the cause, the result was that between three and four hundred buildings were burned down, including Trinity Church. As the fire crept northward up Broadway, it burned everything in its path—everything except St. Paul's Church. Miraculously, even though buildings around it burned to the ground, the little church was spared the flames. When the Revolutionary War ended in 1783, the British evacuated New York City. The devastated city began rebuilding itself, but the process was slow. A new Trinity Church was under construction, but in

April 1789, when Washington took the oath as President, it was not completed. Therefore, after the inauguration at Federal Hall, Washington and the other dignitaries in attendance made their way to St. Paul's Church to give thanks and to pray for guidance in the great endeavor that lay before them. Washington took his place in a specially designed pew and listened quietly to the words from the pulpit. George Clinton, the governor of New York (no relation to Bill), sat across the way in his own personal pew.

Then in 1835, another tragic event took place on Manhattan Island. On the night of December 16, another fire broke out in a warehouse at the southern end of the island. Unlike the fire of 1776, this one was probably an accident caused by an overturned lamp. The fire was fanned by gale-force winds, and the men trying to put it out were impeded by the cold which caused many water sources to freeze. In the end about 700 buildings burned to the ground. Again, Trinity Church was a casualty, but St. Paul's Church withstood the onslaught of the flames. The little church had survived a second devastating fire in New York City, and people began to believe that this church was truly blessed.

Was the church blessed or was it something else? Perhaps it was an unusual guardian angel that saved St. Paul's on at least two occasions, a guardian angel that people did not want to encounter in the wee hours of the morning. Englishman George Frederick Cooke was hailed worldwide as one of the greatest tragedians of the late eighteenth and early nineteenth centuries. But alas, Cooke had a weakness and fondness for drink, which would, on occasion, get the better of him during his performances. Upon his arrival in America in 1810 for a tour of the continent, Cooke found himself in poor health and in need of medical attention. The theater, being more passion than a great income producer, left him unable to pay many of his medical expenses. So, being a creative thespian, he struck up an arrangement with a local hospital. The deal was that in exchange for medical care, he would will his body to science to do with as they pleased.

When George Frederick Cooke died at the age of fifty-six, in 1812, from acute alcoholism, his body did go to science, but the story did not end there. He wound up becoming a major success in Edwin Booth's production of *Hamlet* in the mid-1860s. The only catch was that his "skull" became the showstopper. ("Alas poor Yorick. I knew him, Horatio.") It seems that when Cooke was buried in the graveyard of St. Paul's Church, his head did not find its way into the coffin. Ever since that time, stories circulated that Cooke's body roamed the cemetery, at night, looking for his head, and that he was protecting the church and its grounds until his quest ended and he could finally rest in peace.

Maybe that was the reason that St. Paul's Church was spared on September 11, 2001, or maybe it was for another reason. On that fateful day and for months following the tragedy, the church became the epicenter for the Ground Zero workers including firefighters, EMS workers, police officers, sanitation workers, and just average citizens trying to help. It was here that they could take a breather from the arduous work of looking first for survivors and then for victims of the disaster. Cots were set up on the floor for the workers to rest for a few hours. Food was brought in from different venues all across the city, ranging from local delis to the finest restaurants, to make sure that the workers were well fed before they returned to the site and the task at hand. St. Paul's was also the site, immediately after the tragedy, where people posted pictures of their loved ones in hopes that someone had seen them alive after the Towers fell. It was later the place where signs, flags, banners, badges, and stuffed animals from all around the world were hung to memorialize those who perished on that day.

St. Paul's Church now stands as a memorial to the victims and as a tribute to the workers of the September 11 tragedy. There is even a commemorative to the lone casualty at St. Paul's, the sycamore tree that was felled by a falling steel beam, and a memorial bell in the graveyard paying homage to those who lost their lives. Maybe that was the reason why St. Paul's Church was spared on that day. Maybe it was left standing there so that we will never forget.

A TIGER STROLLS THROUGH
THE URBAN JUNGLE OF QUEENS

2004

It was a beautiful summer day. People were outside picnicking, joggers were jogging, and children were excited because the Cole Brothers Circus, which billed itself as "The World's Largest Circus under a Big Top" (a quote that would make the famous P. T. Barnum roll in his grave), was in town.

This Florida-based traveling circus made a deal to come to Forest Park, Queens, the 538-acre park built in 1890 complete with beautiful trails, biking, golfing, a band shell for concerts, playing fields, a wooden merry-go-round and plenty of room to house this kind of show.

Featured in this circus were the normal array of unusual characters: bendable acrobats; prancing poodles; jugglers on stilts; trick horseback riders; motorcycle daredevils; hat-wearing performing elephants; a Siamese supercat, Rincon, who jumps fifty feet in the air and lands on a pillow; and, of course, beautiful white Bengal tigers.

On this particular day, July 31, 2004, the performers were all getting ready for their Saturday afternoon show. Acrobats were limbering their incredible bodies, trapeze artists were taking a last swing or two before the audiences were brought in, and the animals were getting placed in preparation for the show.

One tiger, a seven-and-a-half-year-old, 450-pound male named Apollo, apparently was getting rather bored with the whole circus thing. Perhaps he longed for days of freedom. Around 1:00 p.m., while he was being transferred from a small cage to a large one to go backstage, the locking mechanism on two cages separated, creating a space for him to get out.

He had a choice: stay and do another show, which he had done hundreds of times, or take a stroll outside and check out the urban jungles of Queens. He chose the latter.

What happened next became a scene out of *Madagascar*. It took a few minutes before any of the circus people noticed what happened. One of his trainers, Cheryl Haddad, tried to stop Apollo from taking his stroll, but it only made Apollo pick up the pace, determined to check out the real estate in the borough of Queens.

Without the aid of a GPS or tourist guide map, Apollo made up his own route. He strolled through the park where he was spotted by a group of Baptist Church choir members having a picnic. He looked at them. They looked at him. In typical New York reaction, one choir member said, "I'm thinking, what a pretty animal. It's my first taste of a safari." Not, "Oh my gosh, there is a tiger on the loose," or "man, that is a wild animal." Just a casual observation, and then she went back to her picnicking. After all, she said, "He was just strolling along, he didn't bother anybody." He continued to stroll through the wooded park, taking in the scenery on his lazy Saturday afternoon walk, with not a care in the world.

Apollo then decided to take the Myrtle Avenue entrance ramp to the Jackie Robinson parkway. He then cut through some woods and followed a hiking path up to a hole in a chain-link fence on Eighty-eighth Lane near Myrtle Avenue.

He jogged along the parkway for a brief moment but apparently didn't like the traffic any more than any New Yorker does and headed for a residential area. He then found some grassy area and laid down to rest.

Unfortunately, the sight of a white tiger jogging on the parkway is not an everyday occurrence, and it caused some motorists to stare. One driver hit the brakes to avoid hitting this beautiful behemoth and wound up causing a five-car collision. No one at the time appeared to be hurt.

By this time the police had been inundated with calls that there was a tiger on the loose in Queens. Not having much formal training in tiger chasing and capture, the police had a plan to surround the beast. Armed with shotguns and tranquilizers, six policemen cornered the animal with drawn guns, creating a perimeter around it until a rolling cage could be brought to take him back to the circus. By then Apollo was bored again. Either that or he wasn't sure how to handle a New York City holdup. As one onlooker later told the *New York Post*, "He was just lying in the bushes. He looked exhausted." New York City can do that to you.

When the trainers showed up with the cage, according to John Durkin of the Police Department Emergency Services, Apollo "looked left, it looked right. It didn't look like it wanted to go into its cage. There were a couple of tense seconds." But his trainer managed to coax him back into his cage with a hand signal. The tiger responded, jumped back into his cage, and was returned safely back to the circus.

The whole half-mile stroll lasted a mere half hour. He didn't perform that afternoon, and one six-year-old customer was very disappointed: "It's corny if they have no tigers."

The media, of course, had a field day. Over 250 stories about Apollo's stroll appeared in papers and television stations around the globe.

The circus got slapped with a health code summons. Not much of a penalty, especially considering this was the second time their animals chose to make a break for freedom before a show. Back in July of 1995, Tina and Jewel, their resident performing elephants, broke loose in Forest Park, trampled a parked car, and knocked over seven people. Apollo was obviously a lot more sedate in his stroll.

Nonetheless, word of this new escape got out to NY State Senator Carl Kruger, who was against the Cole Brothers Circus for years. He said it compounded the "Flying Cat cruelty finding" (in which the Cole brothers were being fined for making a Siamese Cat jump/fall fifty feet through the air and land on a pillow), in addition to many other violations that Cole Brothers had been slapped with in regards to animal cruelty. He said that this was one more reason not to allow that circus and their bag of tricks to come to the boroughs.

Others of course just wanted to cash in on the tiger's stroll. Several years later, on January 7, 2009, a Brooklyn court awarded two drivers who were on the Robinson Parkway that day $935,000 in damages, which was to be paid by the trainer Josef Marcan. The drivers, an off-duty New York Police officer and a Queens woman who will split the cash, claimed they had suffered devastating back injuries in the chain-reaction crash, even though at the time the injuries were characterized as minor by a spokesperson for the police department's public information office.

They say curiosity kills a cat; in this case, it just cost his trainer a million bucks. Either way, Apollo had a story to tell his other animal counterparts. And I'm sure when his cage rolls by Tina and Jewel's he winks as if to say, "We've seen the outside world and we like it."

NEW YORK CITY TRIVIA

- On July 26, 1788 New York became the eleventh state.

- New York got its name from the Duke of York.

- Between all the taxi drivers they speak sixty languages.

- Its official sister city is Tokyo—10,870 miles away.

- NYC was the capital of the United States from 1783 to 1789.

- Mayor Fiorello LaGuardia spoke seven languages, including fluent Yiddish; his mother was Jewish.

- Winston Churchill's mother, Jenny, was an American from the wealthy Jerome family (Jerome Avenue in the Bronx).

- The Waldorf Astoria Hotel in Manhattan is built on shock absorbers to reduce the vibrations from the trains that travel under it; flags hanging outside the hotel indicate that a foreign VIP is present inside.

- In Manhattan, odd-numbered streets run west, and even-numbered streets run east.

- In 1701 there was an English governor of New York, Lord Cornbury (Edward Hyde), who was a cross-dresser; he also once owned Hyde Park, Franklin Roosevelt's home.

- Fifth Avenue is the dividing line between the West Side and the East Side.

- The Statue of Liberty's face is the sculptor's mother and the body is his mistress; the interior was done by Gustav Eiffel (the Eiffel Tower builder).

- On Twenty-third Street and Fifth Avenue, there is a statue of William Seward, Lincoln's Secretary of State who bought Alaska (Seward's Folly). A problem arose when constructing the statue; the sculptor ran out of funds, so he took an extra Lincoln body and welded Seward's head on top. Lincoln was six feet four inches, and Seward was five feet two inches—not even close!

- There are more people buried in the Borough of Queens (3 million) than living in Queens (2.3 million).

- If a subway station displays a green globe, that station runs twenty-four hours; if the globe is red, that station is closed.

- DUMBO means Down Under the Manhattan Bridge Overpass.

- NOHO means North of Houston Street.

- SOHO means South of Houston Street.

- The constellations on the ceiling in Grand Central Terminal are backward.

- The "Naked Cowboy" in Times Square, Robert John Burck II, professes to make $700–$1,000 a day posing in his underwear.

- The "Dakota Building" is a nickname because when it was built in 1884, there was nothing around, so you might as well have been living in the Dakota Territory.

- Grant is not buried in Grant's Tomb; he is entombed aboveground.

- The Tavern on the Green Restaurant in Central Park was once the home for the sheep that grazed in the Park.

- New York City was once the second largest slave market in America, just behind Charleston, South Carolina.

- Pearl Street was named for the oyster shells that washed up on land in the early days of New York City.

- William Sidney Porter, who wrote "The Gift of the Magi" at Pete's Tavern, wrote under the pen name O. Henry, which came from the time that he spent in the *Oh*io P*en*iteni*ary*.

- There are estimated to be between 10,000 and 20,000 people buried under Washington Square Park.

- In Old English, "wich" is "village," so technically Greenwich Village is "Green Village Village."

- The Museum of Sex on Twenty-seventh Street and Fifth Avenue used to have a sign in its front window that read PLEASE DO NOT TOUCH, LICK, STROKE, OR MOUNT THE EXHIBITS.

- Forty-seventh Street used to be known as "the Street of Krapp" after Herbert J. Krapp, who designed many of the theaters there.

- The terms "Broadway," "Off-Broadway," and "Off-off Broadway" have nothing to do with location; it's based on size of the theater. Broadway has over 500 seats, Off-Broadway from 100 to 499 seats, and Off-off Broadway 99 seats and below.

- The statue at the Rockefeller Center Ice Rink of Prometheus was nicknamed "Leaping Louie" by the press.

- The statue of Atlas on Fifth Avenue opposite St. Patrick's Cathedral, was the scene of a protest when unveiled in 1937; people thought it looked too much like the Italian dictator Mussolini.

- On Christmas Eve in 1908, Mayor George B. McClellan Jr. ordered all 550 nickelodeon movie theaters to close and revoked licenses, leaving 12,000 people instantly unemployed. His reasoning was that the people who ran the movies were without scruples. It was forbidden to show any tragedy, comedy, opera, ballet, farce, dancing, wrestling, jugglers, acrobats, vaudeville shows, singing, impersonations, or any parts of plays. Theater owners fought back and the theaters were reopened, proving you could fight city hall.

NEW YORK CITY'S WORLD RECORDS AND FIRSTS

- One of the authors, Fran Capo, is in the *Guinness Book of World Records* as the world's fastest talking female. She was born in New York City, ran the New York City Marathon, and got Mayor Edward Koch (along with the help of her comedy buddy Alan Chan) to proclaim December 12, 1985, as the first official Comedy Day in New York City.

- The Williamsburg Savings Bank Building in Brooklyn has the world's largest clock on the top. Each of the clock's four sides has a diameter of twenty-seven feet.

- Broadway is the longest city street in the world. It stretches 150 miles between Bowling Green in Manhattan to Albany, New York.

- Gravesend, once a separate village in Brooklyn, was the first colony founded by a woman, Lady Deborah Moody, in 1643.

- The first crossword puzzle appeared on December 2, 1913, in the *New York World.*

- The world's first hotel to have an elevator was the Fifth Avenue Hotel in 1859.

- The *Guinness Book of World Records'* most versatile man, Ashrita Furman, lives in Queens, New York. He has broken (at the time of this writing) 244 world records, more than any other human alive.

- St. John the Divine is the largest cathedral in the city and the world. It's located on Amsterdam Avenue at West 112th Street. The nave of the cathedral is 601 feet high.

- The world's first science museum for the young was founded in 1899. It is the Brooklyn Children's Museum at 145 Brooklyn Avenue.

- The first New York City Marathon was run in 1970 and was a series of laps around Central Park.

BIBLIOGRAPHY

Applegate, Debby. *The Most Famous Man in America.* New York: Doubleday, 2006. (1995)

Baker, Paul R. *Stanny: The Golden Life of Stanford White.* New York: Free Press Division of Macmillan Press, 1989.

Ballon, Hilary and Kenneth Jackson. *Robert Moses and the Modern City: The Transformation of New York.* New York: W.W. Norton and Company, 2007.

Cotter, Bill and Bill Young. *The 1964–1965 New York World's Fair.* Chicago: Arcadia Publishing, 2004.

Eells, George and Stanley Musgrove. *Mae West.* New York: William Morrow and Company, Inc., 1982.

Ellis, Robb. *The Epic of New York.* New York: Kanadosha Press, 2004.

Fischler, Stan. *Uptown Downtown: A Trip through Time on New York's Subways.* New York: Hawthorn Books, 1976.

Gage, Beverly. *The Day Wall Street Exploded: A Story of America in its First Age of Terror.* New York: Oxford University Press, 2009.

Goldsmith, Barbara. *Other Powers.* New York: Harper Perennial, 1998.

Jackson, Kenneth. *The Encyclopedia of New York.* New York: Columbia University Press, 1995.

Janvier, Thomas. *In Old New York.* New York: St. Martin's Press, 2000.

BIBLIOGRAPHY

Kert, Bernice. *Abby Aldrich Rockefeller.* New York: Random House, 2003.

Ketchum, Richard M. *Divided Loyalties.* New York: Henry Holt and Company, 2002.

Lockwood, Charles. *Manhattan Moves Uptown: The Illustrated History.* New York: Barnes and Noble Books, 1995.

MacCracken, Henry Mitchell. *The Hall of Fame.* New York: G. P. Putnam's Sons, 1901.

Morris, Lloyd. *Incredible New York.* New York: Random House, 1951.

Roth, Andrew. *Infamous Manhattan.* New York: Citadel Press, 1996.

Shulman, Irving. *Valentino.* New York: Trident Press, 1967.

INDEX

ABOUT THE AUTHORS

Fran Capo is a cohost of the television show *Live it Up! With Donna Drake and Fran Capo.* She is also a comedienne, spokesperson, adventurer, voice-over artist, freelance writer, and the author of ten additional books. This Queens College graduate is also a keynote motivational speaker and is hired to do her lectures—Dare to Do It, Creativity in Marketing, Humor in Business Speaking, and Success Made Simple—for Fortune 500 companies, corporate promotional events, colleges, schools, and fund-raisers. Fran has been heard on over 350 television shows and 3,500 radio shows, and is a cohost on the national radio show *Comedy Cures Laugh Talk Radio.* She also writes a weekly blog, "Adventure Mom," for http://travelingmom.com.

Fran is the proud mother of Spencer Patterson and holds five world records; the best-known is the world's fastest talking female (you may recognize her voice from the national XM-Sirius radio commercial). Her other world records include the highest book signing (at the top of Mt. Kilimanjaro); the deepest book signing (at the wreck site of the *Titanic*—yes, she actually went down there; only 108 people in the world have done that; more people have been to outer space!); Chiromission, where she joined 39 chiropractors and saw 21,595 patients in two days; and for the fastest song published from concept to national broadcast for her theme song, "Adventure Girl." Fran is listed in *Guinness, Ripley's,* and *The Record Holder Republic's* world record books. She also does a fast-talking celebrity tour of New York City with her coauthors, the Zuckermans. If you are interested in booking Fran for an event, she can be reached via e-mail at FranCNY@aol.com, or visit her Web site, www.francapo.com. You can also follow her on Twitter and Facebook.

Susan and Art Zuckerman live in New Rochelle, New York, with their two sons and two golden retrievers, and have previously appeared on TV shows such as *ITV London, BBC London, Inside Edition, The Travel Channel (Central Park and Chinatown), Japanese Animal Planet,* and ZDF German TV. They also host *"Z" Travel and Leisure* for WVOX Radio in New York and are reporters for a local newspaper chain writing about NYC. You can hear them live by visiting www.ztravelandleisure.com and clicking on "Listen Live."

Susan and Art are both licensed tour guides and are certified by New York State to teach teachers New York City history and culture for college and graduate credit. Currently, Susan is an adjunct professor at Monroe College specializing in teaching New York City History. Their passion for NYC allows them to conduct tours of NYC history and offer unique food tours of NYC. They are also the historians for the landmark Hall of Fame for Great Americans. They have an extensive book collection of over 15,000 books and love showing off the city to guests!